DREAMS

MW01076539

DREAMS AND
PREMONITIONS

PSYCHIC PHENOMENA

First Edition 1916
L W Rogers

New Edition 2019
Edited by Tarl Warwick

COPYRIGHT AND DISCLAIMER

FOREWORD

This little work is the result of the mind of LW Rogers; once a socialist and labor "activist" turned Theosophist- a fairly prolific writer and an orator to boot. For its era, it is quite in depth and some degree of rigor and accuracy attends it, particularly the passages that refer to remembering dreams using the simple (and still-utilized) method of writing down the content in the morning as soon as physically able.

The concept of premonitions is still believed in today; I have had them frequently myself albeit in strictly symbolic form; they do defy, in my own opinion, a truly rational explanation at least within the framework of rational thought currently employed by the mainstream of society. While this work openly opposes the idea of the mind delivering them via some deeper reasoning in symbolic form, it is one that is at least potentially acceptable even in a secular capacity.

The large number of anecdotes related here in which premonitions are present is rather impressive; it explicitly speaks of one tale from the Messina quake (in Italy, 1908) involving the discovery of a sailors' lover after he had a dream regarding her location. This particular, albeit short, passage is quite interesting; other such stories are related, also.

This edition of "Dreams and Premonitions" has been carefully edited for format and content. Care has been taken to retain all original intent and meaning.

DREAMS AND PREMONITIONS

INTRODUCTION

Dreams and premonitions are the most common of all psychic phenomena, but they are nevertheless but little understood. Modern psychology has accumulated an immense array of facts which very conclusively show that the consciousness of the human being is something vaster, deeper and altogether more remarkable than has generally been supposed. But just there the psychologists stop, on the very threshold of great discoveries. They are puzzled by the remarkable facts and are baffled in their attempts to co-relate them and satisfactorily explain them.

The facts that have been collected and verified show that while some dreams are fantastic, contradictory and illogical, others are not only coherent and logical, but present a marvelous depth of wisdom which, when compared to ordinary human knowledge, seems almost like omniscience. They sometimes solve problems that are impossible of solution by the waking consciousness, and frequently actually forecast the future by accurately describing an event which has not yet occurred but which is to be. Thus people have dreamed of their approaching death, or of the death of others, stating exactly the nature of the accident that would cause it, and describing in detail the scenes of the coming tragedy. Yet again the impending event presented to the consciousness in the dream state may represent only the most trivial of circumstances.

Sometimes dreams give warnings about dangers that are threatening but of which the waking consciousness is wholly oblivious. In other cases a dream has enabled one to become a rescuer and lifesaver in some approaching disaster. Occasionally in a dream accurate knowledge is obtained of some tragedy that

4

is occurring at a distance, or of a crime that has been committed, while again missing people have been located and lost objects have been recovered through dreams.

The truth of these astounding facts is beyond all question. The problem is to explain the facts. Modern psychology talks rather vaguely of the subconscious mind and of the subliminal self, but this really explains nothing. We do not advance toward the understanding of a mystery simply by applying to it a new name. What is that thing called the subconscious, or the subliminal, and what are its powers and its limitations? Unless science can satisfactorily answer such questions it has done little indeed toward solving these psychological puzzles. The most striking characteristic of the recent work of writers on dreams is the strong tendency toward a purely materialistic interpretation of the phenomena observed. Hampered by the wholly inadequate hypothesis that dreams are caused either by impressions made on the physical senses or by desires of the waking consciousness, they fill their pages with a discussion of the class of dreams that may thus be explained and carefully avoid the dreams that are really worthy of investigation just because they present facts that no such hypothesis can dispose of. It is some cause for congratulation, however, that after devoting much space to a description of the dreams which illustrate the well-known fact that slight external stimuli often cause exaggerated brain impressions- as, for example, a drop of water on the face causing a dream of a violent rainstorm- these writers often devote a closing paragraph to the admission that neither physical nor mental causes are sufficient to account for the dreams that occasionally forecast the future. Now, it is precisely those occasional dreams which the materialistic hypothesis can not explain that it is important to understand, for they alone can give some clue to the real nature of human consciousness. We shall surely learn but little by going many times over the beaten path of admitted facts while neglecting to look beyond to the unexplored fields so full of fascinating possibilities.

The merest glance is sufficient to show that there are two distinct classes of dreams; that one class constitutes a memory, on awakening, of something that is related to impressions made on the physical senses; that the other class clearly has no such origin and that, instead of being distorted and fantastic, such dreams sometimes embody profound wisdom or accurate knowledge of future events. These two classes of dreams no more arise from the same causes than the noise made by the revolving record of a phonograph has the same origin as the song of intelligence and emotion that flows from it. The one is purely mechanical, while the other is purely mental and spiritual, transmitted through a material mechanism. And that is the true distinction between the dream arising from a physical cause and the dream which owes its origin to the higher activities of unfettered consciousness.

The one is produced by the mechanism of consciousness- the physical brain and its etheric counterpart- automatically responding to external stimuli and putting together fragmentary brain pictures. The other is the result of the activity of the ego impressing the physical brain with transcendental truth. Psychologists should not be slower than the most progressive of physical scientists in accepting the fact of clairvoyance and recognizing the part it plays in occult research. There is so much of reliable evidence on record involving the use of clairvoyance that it would be almost as much a waste of time to argue its existence as to contend that there is a state of consciousness known as trance. Those who are familiar with the clairvoyant faculty and with the remarkable powers of the scientifically trained clairvoyant, will need no argument to convince them that here is a means of ascertaining the truth about the various states of consciousness and their relationship to the physical mechanism through which they are expressed.

DREAMS AND PREMONITIONS

But it is of secondary importance whether the reality of clairvoyance be admitted or denied; for from the phenomena clairvoyantly observed and cataloged it is possible to construct the hypothesis that will explain the facts, and all of the known facts, related to dreams. Any hypothesis that can do that legitimately holds its place, and must be regarded as sound until a fact is produced that it can not explain.

The method of acquiring the knowledge from which a hypothesis is constructed is of little importance. The only question to be considered is whether the hypothesis can explain the admitted facts. On its ability to do that it must stand or fall. There is a working hypothesis that logically and satisfactorily explains all the remarkable facts, tragic or trivial, presented by dreams and premonitions; that will enable us to classify and comprehend them; that will assign to each dream neither less nor more importance than the facts warrant, and that will give to those interested in the subject a key to these mysteries of the mind. The purpose of the following chapters is to present this hypothesis, together with the necessary facts to fully illustrate the psychic principles involved in the remarkable dreams herein recorded.

CHAPTER I

The Dreamer

Before we can hope to comprehend dreams we must understand the nature and constitution of the dreamer. We must free ourselves of some of our materialistic conceptions and consider the question of what the human being really is. It is the popular error of regarding man as being nothing more than a physical body and brain that has so sadly retarded progress in this field of research. The very phenomena with which psychology deals should long ago have destroyed such an untenable premise, for by that materialistic hypothesis it is utterly impossible to account for the facts in hand.

The work of such scientists as Crookes and Lodge and Richet has finally turned public attention in the right direction. They have presented evidence in overwhelming abundance to show that the consciousness is not dependent on the physical body for its continuity; that after bodily death the consciousness survives, and that during the life of the physical body the consciousness may also function quite independently of it. So conclusive are the facts gathered by varied and long-continued experiments that Sir Oliver Lodge was led to declare in a lecture before the Society For The Advancement of Science that the. continent of a new world had been discovered, and that already a band of daring investigators had landed on its treacherous but promising shores.

This new "continent" belongs, of course, to the invisible world, and these pioneers of the scientific army are not the first to explore it. They are only the vanguard of the physical scientists. The occult scientists were long ahead of them, and had explored and studied the invisible realms. Naturally enough they hail the advent of the physical scientists with the greatest

8

satisfaction, for they are rapidly confirming what the occultists long have taught about the constitution of man. It is only when we have fully before us these facts about the real nature of man, and understand that he is essentially a spiritual being, a minor part only of whose energies come into action in the material realms, that we shall be able to comprehend the phenomena of dreams and premonitions. Let us turn our attention, then, to the occult side of the problem and examine the working hypothesis that satisfactorily explains the facts.

This hypothesis is that the human being is an individualized portion of the universal mind which, in turn, is but one expression of the Supreme Being; that man is "an image of God" in the very literal sense of having potentially within him the attributes, the power and the wisdom of the deity to which he is thus so directly related; that his evolution is going forward in a world that has both its spiritual and physical regions; that he is essentially a soul ,or center of consciousness, functioning through a physical body which is but the temporary vehicle of the real man in the same sense that an automobile is one's vehicle, and that this material body- which is in reality but the clothing of the soul, as the glove is the clothing of the hand- is discarded at death without in any degree affecting the life and consciousness that has temporarily used it for gaining experience in the material realms. Man is, therefore, a soul possessing a material body that enables him to be conscious and active in the physical world. This hypothesis reverses the old materialistic conception completely. This is man's temporary life. He existed as an intelligence before he came down into these material regions through birth in a physical body, and when that body dies he resumes his relationship to his home plane, the spiritual world. But this spiritual world is not merely a realm of thought.

It is a world of form and a life of activity, of deeper, wider knowledge than the physical, an ethereal world, but still a world of thought, of action and of enterprise. It is a world of tenuous matter, a huge globe, not distant in space but enclosing and interpenetrating our own as the ether, postulated by science, surrounds and interpenetrates all physical objects. It is sometimes called the astral world. This ethereal world as a whole naturally has its sub-divisions, but for the purpose of understanding the phenomena of dreams it is not necessary to introduce details. It is necessary, however, to comprehend the relationship between the physical and astral regions, and between the physical and astral portions of the mechanism of consciousness. The relationship of the former is that of a world within a world- the astral globe being composed of matter so tenuous that it encloses the physical globe, interpenetrates it throughout, and extends far beyond it in space. As a ball of fibrous matter might be immersed in liquid matter, saturated with it, and completely surrounded by it, so the physical globe is interpenetrated and enveloped by the matter of the astral world. The astral world, then, is not remote but is here in the midst of us, about us, through us and beyond us.

The relationship of the physical and astral bodies of a human being are of a like nature. The tenuous matter of the astral body is within and without the physical body, extending somewhat beyond it, and constituting an exact duplicate of it: Of course; neither of these bodies is in any sense the man. Both are parts of the complex mechanism through which he manifests himself, and the astral body is a higher and fuller expression of the man than the physical body is. Indeed, the latter is merely the body of action. It is only the instrument of the man, which enables him to be present in the physical world, while the astral body is that with which he feels and through which thought and emotion are sent downward, or outward, into the physical body. The physical body has no part in the generation of thought. It is merely the means by which thought and emotion are expressed in the material world. Therefore, thought and emotion do not come to an end when the physical body is inactive on account of either sleep or death.

DREAMS AND PREMONITIONS

These two encasements of the real man- the physical and astral bodies- separate from each other under certain conditions, the latter being used as a vehicle of consciousness while the former is quiescent. A diver uses a boat and a diver's suit. Both are necessary for the work he is to do. But he may leave the boat and use only the diving suit for a time. The boat served the purpose of enabling him to go from point to point on the surface. The diving suit enables him to explore a region in which the boat is not available. Neither is the man. They are merely the mechanism that he uses. So it is with his visible and invisible bodies. The visible physical body may be discarded and the invisible astral body may then be used as the vehicle of the consciousness, or soul- the man himself- in the more ethereal regions.

But what are the conditions under which the consciousness withdraws from the physical body and functions through the astral body? One is sleep and the other is death. Sleep always indicates the separation of the visible from the invisible body. Whether the sleep is natural, or is induced by hypnotism or trance, it indicates the reparation of the bodies. There can be no such separation without sleep and no sleep without such separation. Sleep is simply the absence of the man from his physical body. That is why it is asleep. It is not being used by the man. His intelligence is not flowing through it. He is not there.

But how, then, it may be asked, does the breathing continue and the heart beat if the body is without its tenant? How does the worm entombed within the chrysalis become the butterfly? How do creatures below the line of intellect in the evolutionary scale live without thinking? Our physical bodies are not dependent upon our intellects. We do not consciously direct the beating of the heart nor the processes of digestion during the waking hours. The activities necessary to the life and well-being of the body go on until its death whether we think of them or do

11

not, and whether the consciousness is functioning through the body or is withdrawn from it.

Death is the other cause of the separation of the astral body from the physical body, and the only difference between sleep and death is that in sleep the man withdraws his consciousness temporarily from the physical body and later returns to it. The act of withdrawing is what we call falling asleep. Returning is what we call awakening. The instant the consciousness is withdrawn the physical body is asleep. That is what sleep is- the separation of the astral body from the physical body. The soul, the real man, has temporarily laid down his instrument of activity in the visible world. It is then like a vacant house with drawn curtains until its absent tenant returns to it, and begins to send his consciousness through it. During his absence he has been using his astral body as his vehicle of consciousness, just as the diver temporarily abandoned his boat for his diving suit.

In death the consciousness has been withdrawn from the physical body for the last time. The absence is permanent. The body has worn out or has been injured beyond the possibility of repair. The soul, the real man, can not return to it because it no longer serves the purpose for which it came into existence. It is a worthless machine, worn out through long use, broken suddenly by violence or wasted slowly by disease, as the case may be. During all the temporary absences called sleep there was a magnetic connection between the astral and physical bodies of the man. But when death comes the tie between the soul and the material bod)' is broken and there is no possibility of returning to it. And that is what death is- the severing of the bond between the visible and invisible bodies. The physical body is then dead and disintegration begins. But the real man, the individual consciousness, has not ceased to live. He has merely lost the instrument that connected him with the material world, and which enabled him to move about on it and be known to others there. He is physically dead because he has lost the physical body.

He is not mentally and emotionally dead because he has not lost that part of his mechanism of consciousness which is the seat of thought and emotion. The physical body enabled him to express his life in the visible world but it was no more the man than a phonograph is the person who sings into it. If the phonograph is broken the only change to the singer is that he has lost the instrument of his expression, not his consciousness.

It may, at first thought, seem grotesque to speak of a man as possessing more than one body. Being to many an unaccustomed thought it may sound as bizarre as to say that a person may occupy two houses at one and the same time. But nevertheless the idea represents scientific accuracy. As a matter of fact we do live in two houses whenever we live in any house. Science asserts that every physical atom has its duplicate in etheric matter, by which it is surrounded and interpenetrated. Every building, every brick and board, has its counterpart in unseen matter. The immobile mountains, the flowing streams, the swaying tree-tops, the waving fields of grain, the placid lakes and the ocean tempest tossed, all have their exact counterparts in the invisible matter that reproduces the world in phantom form.

So much science is able to demonstrate and the very nature of this truth compels us to postulate still other and rarer grades of matter than the ether. It is the next rarer grade of invisible matter that the scientists almost brought within the catalog of ascertained facts by discovering the electron and proving that the atom is a minute universe in itself. When we hold a pebble in the hand we do not see all of the pebble. It consists of its visible and invisible parts, and sight and touch can deal with but one of them. The trained clairvoyant would see what others see and also the grades of subtle matter surrounding it and interpenetrating it. Now, since this surrounding and interpenetrating relationship of seen and unseen matter is as true of one object as another, the physical body is no exception. Duplicating it exactly in form and feature is the tenuous matter of a rarer grade, surrounding and permeating it. The consciousness functions through these two bodies as one complex instrument, yet they are separable. An aeroplane is equipped for movement both on the ground and through the air. It may lose its wheels without losing its power to soar. It has merely lost that part of its mechanism that enabled it to operate in connection with the grosser element. So with man. When he loses his physical body it limits his field of activities but does not change the man himself nor impair his ability to function elsewhere.

The dreamer, then, is vastly more than a physical body with a mysterious brain. We are not dealing with a machine, a portion of which "secretes thought as the liver secretes bile," as a scientist of a past generation ventured to guess, but with a spiritual being functioning through a material body containing a brain that is at once an instrument of thought and a limitation of consciousness; for if thought and emotion have a superphysical origin a large percentage of their original energy must be expended in attaining material expression. Therefore the dreamer, in his waking hours, is expressing but a faint reflection of his true consciousness, which is necessarily limited by its material media. As a fragment of the universal mind he- possesses within his unfettered self a wisdom wholly foreign to his physical existence. The home plane of his being is above the limitations of those conditions of consciousness which we know as time and space. He is temporarily blinded by matter while functioning through the material body. He identifies himself with it and loses conscious connection with his higher estate. But when he escapes the limitations of the physical body, either in sleep or in death, and begins to function through his astral body he is a stage nearer to reality and has, in some degree, a transcendental grasp of human affairs. In the case of

DREAMS AND PREMONITIONS

sleep he returns, at the moment of awakening, from the higher state of consciousness to the lower level of physical plane consciousness and is again subjected to the limitations of the physical brain. But the physical brain has its counterpart in astral matter and it is the astral form in which the consciousness, the real man, has been functioning during the hours of sleep. His experiences during that time have given rise to thoughts and emotions which are not impressed upon the physical brain because it has had no part in them. They have set up vibrations only in the subtler portions of the mechanism of consciousness. Ordinarily upon the re-uniting of the astral and physical bodies the vibrations of the tenuous astral matter are not communicated to the matter of the physical brain and there is no memory of what has occurred during the period of slumber. Occasionally, however, there is a rare combination of physical, astral and mental, conditions that makes memory possible and the recollection is called a dream. But all memories of the sleeping hours are not recollections of astral events and it is only after some effort and experience that it becomes possible to distinguish between the memories which represent the adventures of the soul in the astral region and the brain pictures caused by the automatic activity of the physical brain, in which external stimuli sometimes play a most dramatic part.

Nevertheless the two distant classes of dreams, those caused by automatic physiological activity, occasionally associated with excitation outside the body, and those which represent the experiences of the man himself in the ethereal realms, are, as analysis will show, as different in their characteristics as are the causes which produce them.

CHAPTER II

The Materialistic Hypothesis Is Inadequate

Some modern writers have labored mightily to show that dreams may be explained by a purely materialistic hypothesis. Coincidence has been put under such stress as to raise the accidental to the dignity of the causal. Telepathy has been relied upon to cover a multitude of lame conclusions. To explain strange facts we have been given far-fetched solutions that require more credulity for their acceptance than any fairy tale of our childhood days. A writer will cheerfully set out to give a satisfactory material solution for any and all dreams and will explain that the reason why a certain lady dreamed of the correct number of an unknown address was possibly because she had seen that particular number on the paging of a book the day before! Another relates the story of a dinner party being interrupted by one of their number being suddenly impressed with the feeling that he must go immediately to a barn not far away; that an undefinable "something" was wrong there.

He had no idea what it might be but he had an inner impulsion with the barn as a destination. It was an unreasonable but irresistible impulse to go immediately to examine the barn, and apparently for no reason at all. None of the others shared the feeling but upon reaching the barn they were astonished to find that a small blaze had started in some unknown way and there would have been a conflagration but for their timely arrival. Here we have a phenomenon not easily explained. But it does not trouble the writer who presents it in order to show how simple it all is. "He smelled the smoke!" triumphantly exclaims this Sherlock Holmes of psychic riddles. And when, in such a case, it is shown that the feeling of anxiety positively antedated the starting of the blaze by some minutes he falls back on the final resort of the "subconscious self," quite overlooking the fact that that is begging the question and really explains nothing.

In one of the leading monthly periodicals a well known psychologist for a time conducted a department on psychology and the announced purpose was to explain away puzzling psychic experiences in daily affairs. The thoughtful reader will find it difficult to believe that the people who propounded the questions were satisfied with the answers but they are apparently the best that modern psychology is prepared to give them. However, if the "solutions" serve no other purpose they are at least useful in illustrating the trivial arguments presented and the astounding conclusions reached. It was not so long ago that the fact of telepathy was struggling for slight recognition and was knocking almost unheard at the door of modern psychology.

Slowly its status changed from the condition of an outcast to tardy recognition of its usefulness, and the rapidly accumulating mass of psychic facts is likely to raise it soon to the importance of becoming the last hope of the ultra-materialist. Our psychologist of the periodical above mentioned had not proceeded far with his department until he opened his monthly digest with this declaration: "In the many letters received by me since I began to discuss psychical problems in these columns, one fact has been increasingly evident- the actuality of telepathy or thought transference. Even if I had started with a disbelief in telepathy- which I assuredly did not- I could not have retained my skepticism after studying the letters my readers have sent me. From every State in the Union, from Canada, England, France, and other European countries, has come evidence, testifying with cumulative force that in some mysterious way one mind can in truth communicate directly with another mind, though half the world apart."

Without the fact of telepathy the attempt of the psychologist to explain some of the dreams submitted would, indeed, put him in hard case; for even with telepathy, and telepathy strained and twisted out of all semblance to its legitimate self, his hypothesis is still hopelessly weak and utterly inadequate. Telepathy- the communication between mind and mind without material means- has been demonstrated by the simple method of one person acting as the "sender" and being handed a written word or a simple drawing upon a piece of paper supplied by the experimenter, who has himself at that moment conceived it. The "sender" fixes his attention upon it.

At that moment another person who is acting as the "receiver," stationed at a distance of, let us say, a hundred miles, waiting with pencil in hand, reproduces the word or drawing with more or less accuracy as the case may be. By the hypothesis laid down in Chapter I the explanation is as simple as wireless telegraphy. Thought is a force as certainly as electricity is a force. When a mental picture is formed in the mind, grades of subtle matter rarer than that of the brain are thrown into vibration and reproduce themselves in the mind of the "receiver" after the fashion of the vibrations initiated by the sending instrument of wireless telegraphy. But telepathy has its limitations as certainly as telegraphy has. A thought, a feeling, a mood, an emotion may be telepathically communicated from one person to another and apparently regardless of any intervening space which the limits of the earth can impose. In the case of people with minds well developed and capable of forming strong and clear mental images a more extended communication would conceivably be possible.

The scientific experiments thus far made have, however, resulted in no such accomplishment. The most that can be said to be proved for telepathy is that communication is a truth of nature and that it may occur in cases where, although the parties are widely separated, there is either strong effort to communicate or where there is a bond of sympathy between them. When people are together and their minds are running along the same lines it may occur under the most ordinary circumstances. But we must not overlook the part played by facial expression in reading the thoughts of others, nor of the physical conditions that shape thought in a common mold as, for example, when your friend rises to open a window before you can utter the request that is in your mind.

He may have thought of it because he was moved by your thought or only because he, too, was uncomfortable. There are other cases not at all susceptible to such explanation. One often gets telepathically the thought of another who is near him but it is partial and fragmentary. He does not get a complete inventory of the content of the other's mind. So far as casual experience and scientific experiment have gone it has been made fairly clear that while telepathy is common it marks out an extremely narrow field in psychological phenomena. Deprived of the connecting link of personal presence and conversation, or ties of close sympathy, it seems to be effective only when the thought is stimulated by some powerful emotion like sudden and serious illness, accident or death.

When we go beyond that we are in the realm of assumption and speculation. To assume that because one mind can catchy a thought or emotion from another telepathically, one person therefore gets from another's mind without effort or desire all the details relating to something that individual has seen or heard, is as absurd as to assume that because wireless telegraphy brings a message that has passed through the mind of the sending operator the message might in some mysterious way give a knowledge of everything else known to that individual. And yet just such fantastic and groundless assumption is what our psychologist is forced to, in the effort to explain some of the cases submitted. Here is an example:

"A trifle over a year ago, contemplating a trip East, I decided to rent my furnished six-room apartment. It was taken by two young ladies, one employed, the other the home-keeper.

DREAMS AND PREMONITIONS

Some three weeks later I had the most distressing dream. I thought I went over to my apartment, only to find everything in most dreadful confusion. The sun porch had been converted into a temporary bedroom, and in my own bedroom, where usually stood the dressing table (now on the porch) stood a small iron bed, white, with everything upset and dirty. In my dream I also saw that the young ladies had taken in as boarders a married couple with two little ones. Well, I immediately forgot the dream, but several nights later had the same dream again. Imagine my surprise at learning after my return home, that just what I had dreamed had actually occurred, even to the little white bed."

Then follows the psychologist's explanation. He says:

"On the facts as stated this dream must be regarded as telepathic. There is, of course, a possibility that the dreamer, before leaving home, had, without being aware of it, heard her prospective tenants talking about their plans for taking in boarders, changing the furniture, etc. The dream would then be merely the emergence of a subconscious memory."

The theory of telepathy in this case is so obviously inadequate that our psychologist hastens to add that there is another possible explanation and then falls back upon the safe vagueness of the subconscious memory. But is his explanation even within the realm of probability? There may be the possibility, he argues, that she had heard talk of taking in boarders and changing the furniture S But even if that had happened and even if we were to grant some connection between that fact and the dream, how could she have obtained from the knowledge that they would take boarders the fact that the boarders would be a man and his wife and two little children? and if we grant that she unconsciously and in some mysterious way absorbed the information that they would change the furniture, how could that possibly enable her to know that her

20

dressing table would be moved to the porch and that a small white iron bed would be put in its place? There is no evidence, however, that she had heard such conversation, or had the slightest hint that any such thing was contemplated. Indeed, there is good ground for the belief that it was all a most disagreeable surprise to her. She describes the discovery as a "most distressing dream." The reasonable assumption from the language employed by her is that she was astonished and annoyed and was very much disappointed in her tenants. Clearly neither of the explanations of the psychologist really explains this dream.

Our psychologist turns his attention to premonitions with no better results. One of his correspondents submits to him the following experience:

"One Sunday evening during the 'Maine rum war' the pastor of my church announced that Dr. Wilbur F. Krafts, then touring the State in the interests of prohibition, would speak the next day at noon in the public square. Though interested like many others in keeping the prohibitory law, it was by that time, I suppose, 'on my nerves,' and I wanted to hear no more on the subject and left the church as soon as possible. That night I dreamed of returning from my work at noon, hearing the sound of music- 'Marching Through Georgia'- and going to the public square. There I saw a crowd surrounding a group of three or four men. Near the speaker stood my pastor, who, noticing me, made his way through the crowd and spoke to me. At that point I awoke.

"On the forenoon following I had no recollection of my dream and at noon heard music, evidently in the public square. As I started for the square I noticed that the air was 'Marching Through Georgia.' Before I reached the square the music changed to another air as in my dream, which I then remembered. In the square I recognized in Dr. Krafts the speaker of my dream. My pastor was near him and, noticing me, came to me with a message from his wife. Until then I had never seen Dr. Krafts, nor heard anything in particular about him, never had him in mind at all and do not think I had ever seen his picture."

To this the psychologist replies:

"Some psychologists, contrasting the complete forgetfulness until noon with the vividness and fullness of the dream detail recalled by happenings in the square, would insist that the whole dream memory was an unconscious fabrication. But the likelihood is that since, as she says, the prohibition campaign was on her nerves, she did dream something about the meeting to take place the next day. She may easily have dreamed of Dr. Krafts himself for, in spite of her disclaimer, it would be strange indeed if she had never seen a newspaper or poster portrait of him printed in connection with the campaign. If she did dream of Dr. Krafts she would be all the more likely, because of her surprise at recognizing him in the square, to fuse the true details of her dream memory with details of which she had not really dreamed."

Perhaps nothing could appear more absurd to one who has had such an experience than to call it "unconscious fabrication." If that is what such evidence would be called by "some psychologists" they have certainly not been qualified for their work by any personal experience. One of the outstanding facts about such dreams is their vividness and lifelike reality. That she did not remember the dream during the forenoon is no evidence whatever against its reality. What followed was perfectly natural. When she heard the same airs played by the band in the same sequence and saw the same figures she had seen in the dream it is impossible that she could fail to recall it. To say that she may have "fused" the true details of her dream with the details of the events that followed is a far-fetched possibility with no relationship to probability, and a theory is weak indeed that must rely on such an assumption. Akin to it is the hazard that she must have seen Dr. Kraft's picture and forgotten it. Yet if seeing his forgotten picture had enabled her to identify the man, would not seeing the man enable her to remember having previously seen his picture? But the identity of the speaker, which is so unsatisfactorily explained, is of no more importance than the movements of the pastor. In the dream he notices her, comes through the crowd and speaks to her, at which point she awakens. In the events of the next day he does precisely the same thing. There is apparently no sound reason whatever for doubting any part of the evidence.

In another premonitory dream the account runs as follows:

"My mother, an Englishwoman and a deeply religious woman, dreamed she saw my sister lying dead, with two doctors in white beside her. My mother was greatly distressed over this, but as the weeks passed she gradually forgot it, until one day, several months after the dream, my sister had to go to Dublin for a slight operation. Just before commencing they allowed mother to see her and her dream was before her. She recognized it instantly. My sister was unconscious and on the operating table, while a doctor stood on each side."

Which the psychologist thus explains:

"And, no doubt, at the time of the dream the sister's health was such that her mother would consciously or subconsciously be aware that an operation might some day be necessary. Out of this conscious or subconscious knowledge the dream would logically develop, featuring the attending physicians in the regular costume of the operating room." Suppose that for the sake of the argument we were to grant the overworked theory of "subconscious knowledge," and then for good measure were to throw in the admission of the assumption-for which there is no fact in evidence that the daughter's health was bad at the time of the dream. How, even then, can the dream be thus satisfactorily explained? If the mysterious "subconscious knowledge" furnished the information that there would be an operation, then what put two doctors in the dream instead of one, or three? When relatives are admitted to see patients before an operation they usually see them just before the ether is administered. In this instance there must have been some unexpected delay in arriving or some other miscalculation which changed the ordinary course. How did it happen that in the dream the mother saw her daughter apparently dead, lying between the two doctors, with which details the later event exactly corresponded?

If the dream in this case was the waking memory of the ego's dramatization of approaching events it is easy to understand why the mother thought her daughter was dead. Having taken the anesthetic she appeared to lie dead. But if the dream came because the mother was "consciously or subconsciously aware that an operation would sometime be necessary" why did she not dream that her daughter was not dead but had merely taken ether?

None of the explanations of our psychologist will pass the test of analysis. No thoughtful person can fail to observe that, in almost every case, he is obliged to assume facts that are not in evidence, and that he proceeds to build up an imaginary structure and surround the case with conditions which there is no reason to believe really exist. When the facts which are in evidence are antagonistic to his hypothesis he calmly ignores the facts and holds that the witnesses are mistaken! He is a poor attorney who could not win a case were he permitted to be judge and jury as well as advocate.

The ease with which our psychologist can dispose of a difficulty is well illustrated by the following case and explanation:

"My mother tells the following story. When I was several months old she one night put me to sleep in my cradle sound and well as usual, and then went to sleep herself. In the night she was awakened by a dreadful nightmare. She dreamed she was standing over my newly made grave. Getting out of bed, she rushed to my cradle. I was as pale as a sheet, my breath came fast and heavy, and she could not wake me for some time. By the time the doctor arrived I had gone into violent convulsions. My mother to this day says her dream had saved my life. Can you explain it?"

And here is his explanation:

"What undoubtedly had happened was that the noise, however slight, made by the stricken child, had disturbed the watchful mother's sleep, giving rise to the symbolical and most fortunate nightmare."

Now, observe that the child had been put to bed in her usual health. There was nothing to cause the mother the slightest uneasiness. Had the psychologist said that any slight noise made by the child would awaken the mother the statement could easily be accepted. But when he asserts that what must have happened was that some slight noise from the child caused the mother to have a most fortunate nightmare, the statement would be of greater value in the columns of a humorous paper than in a serious study of psychology. The laughable extremity to which our psychologist is pushed in his determination to explain everything from the material viewpoint comes out well in another case which is not a dream at all, but which furnishes a fine example of his method. The experience is stated as follows:

"One summer a party of us were walking along a mountain trail, Indian fashion. I was the last in line, and kept my eyes on the group ahead We came to a clump of trees beside the path. The rest kept right on, but something prompted me to turn to the left and leave the path. I did so, and going around the clump I heard screams, and all ran back. Coiled, ready to strike, was a large rattler that disappeared into the bushes. If I had gone on, instead of around the trees, I should surely have been bitten by the snake."

Then comes his explanation:

"A capital instance, this, of the power of the eye- or, in this case, perhaps the ear- to perceive more than one consciously comprehends, and by this perceiving, to impel to action which seems to be quite without reason and consequently mysterious."

We are here asked to believe that a person sees or hears a rattlesnake near the path, and acts upon the knowledge to avoid the danger without being conscious of the existence of the reptile! Could the demand upon credulity go further than that? One of the most remarkable things about the psychologist of the materialistic type is that while he constantly warns against what he regards as the blind and unreasoning faith of those who see intelligence and purpose in all forces, however apparently chaotic in their expressions, he nevertheless offers explanations of phenomena that set at naught all common sense experience and place an impossible tax upon credulity. A hypothesis accepted by such scientists as Crookes. Lodge, Wallace, Flammarion, Richet and others of equal standing in the scientific world, is disregarded, while, in order to account for all that occurs by the employment of purely physical factors, special conditions are assumed, witnesses are discredited, facts are ignored, and in the name of science conclusions are drawn that represent nothing less than the most arrant nonsense.

With the vague, elusive and undefined "subconsciousness" to fall back upon in an emergency, there is always a safe retreat. And that assurance may be doubly sure our psychologist says:

"Let me urge my readers never to forget that anything which has ever got into the mind, may, under special conditions, be externalized as an hallucination, or may crop up into the recollection in the form of a dream."

When we add to that declaration the privilege of assuming the "special conditions" that may be necessary to make any particular case fit the materialistic interpretation, it certainly ought to go a long way in helping our psychologist to harmonize his theory with the facts! There is no danger of defeat in the arena of logic if there is some byway permitting retirement beyond the reach of logic at any critical moment. Forty years ago when the idea of evolution was getting a foothold in the thought of western civilization I knew an estimable and pious old gentleman whose mind was somewhat scientific in trend but ultra-orthodox in faith. He would not deny a scientific fact or principle, as he understood it, but he clung tenaciously to the old idea of the literal interpretation of the Bible which the evolutionary hypothesis was invalidating, and when he was asked to explain how a certain thing could be so and so, as alleged, when it was in violation of the scientific facts he would reply, "Well, it is the Lord's way." No matter what altogether impossible or utterly contradictory matter had to be explained it was met with the solemn declaration that "It is the Lord's way."

And all the time the old gentleman evidently believed that to be conclusive, and appeared to be serenely unconscious of the fact that anything imaginable can be justified by the man who merely has to declare "it is the Lord's way."

Our psychologist is equally safe. His line of retreat to "subconsciousness" is always open. If a dream accurately forecasts the future it is because the dreamer knew of some fact

27

which, by the wonderful alchemy of the subconsciousness, supplied the future details. If one is in a strange country which he has never before visited, and suddenly becomes aware that it is all as familiar as his own garden, and then proceeds to describe to his friends what lies ahead along the road, it is because he has somewhere had a glimpse of a picture- and forgotten it- and that wonderful subconsciousness accounts for the rest. If one is moving in the darkness toward a precipice a yard away, in perfect ignorance of its existence, and feels himself suddenly bodily pushed backward when there is no living being near him, why, its a hallucination representing ideas latent in his consciousness.

If you are meandering along a forest path, and are suddenly seized with an impulse to leave it for no imaginable reason, and come back to it a few feet further on, and then discover that you thus probably escaped death, it is because your subconsciousness managed the matter. You saw or heard the snake, but didn't know it, or you would have known why you turned aside. If you have a dream of future events as they afterward really transpire, it is only a coincidence unless the details are all in agreement with the dream, and if they are then you didn't dream them; not because you are consciously fabricating, but because the mysterious subconsciousness that previously saved you from snakes is now leading you to "fuse" the details and appear in the role of an unconscious liar; and, finally, if you have a dream that presents facts which cannot possibly be explained by the material hypothesis, you are simply mistaken about it- you only thought you had a dream, because if you really had had such a dream it would not be in agreement with the materialistic theory!

It is, of course, true that some dreams and apparent premonitions can be explained by material facts. It is equally true that a great many dreams can not be thus explained. A close study of them will at once make this apparent and show the utter inadequacy the materialistic hypothesis. Any hypothesis is serviceable only so long as it can explain the known facts. The moment it fails to explain an established fact it falls to the ground, no matter how many other facts it may have satisfactorily explained. The belief that the world was flat and stationary was at one time general. That theory satisfactorily explained the known facts. But when other facts were discovered that could not be thus explained the theory instantly collapsed.

The only question involved was whether there were really new facts to be dealt with. The world discovered that it had been considering only part of the facts. Additional facts destroyed the old hypothesis; and that is precisely the case in the matter here under discussion. The facts have not all been considered. They have either been completely ignored or have been waived aside with the assumption that the most trivial and far-fetched explanations are sufficient to dispose of them. The dreams that are utterly beyond explanation by the materialistic hypothesis constitute evidence as reliable as the others, and are furnished by witnesses who differ in no way from those who have furnished the details of the few dreams that involve no superphysical factors. A glance at some of these dreams will show how hopelessly the old theory breaks down in their presence. Many of them are dreams of discovery which bring to light that which is lost and under circumstances that eliminate telepathy and vague hints at subconscious possibilities. Others are in the nature of warnings of impending danger which does not exist at the time the warning is given.

Sometimes they enable the dreamer after awakening to give life-saving assistance to other people. The fact that some dreams can be fully and satisfactorily explained on purely material grounds does not throw a single ray of light upon the mystery of other dreams in which the dreamer obtains detailed knowledge of what transpired during the night at a distance, or the dream that foreshadows an approaching tragedy.

CHAPTER III

Dreams of Discovery

Most people who are able to give testimony upon such matters are unwilling to be personally mentioned for a double reason; they dread the possible ridicule of the unthinking, and they dislike the task of replying to letters of inquiry which the publicity of the facts may call out. Fortunately there are some who, in the interest of truth, are willing to be witnesses for it regardless of the unpleasantness involved. The extremely interesting and remarkable dream selected to open this chapter was related to me by Mrs. Reeves Snyder, a well-known resident of Springfield, Ohio, with permission to use her name. Her mother had died rather suddenly after a short illness. When the time arrived for adjusting the financial accounts it was discovered that certain bonds were missing. They were not in the strong box at the bank where they were supposed to be, nor had any member of the family the slightest knowledge that could lead to their recovery. They well knew that they would not have been disposed of without their consent and advice.

Every conceivable nook and cranny of the house was searched and re-searched, but the mystery of the missing bonds remained unsolved. The loss was a large one, and as time passed without developing the slightest clue to the missing property the daughter's anxiety grew. One night Mrs. Reeves Snyder dreamed. She found herself in the presence of her dead mother, who smilingly said, "Don't worry any more about those bonds, you'll find them in the morning. I had them at the house just before I was taken ill, and had them in my hand when I went up to the garret floor, and laid them aside while busy there. I forgot them when leaving- and then came the illness and confusion that followed. But they are there, and you will find them in an old tomato can, covered with a board, near the end of the large black trunk."

Awakening, the dreamer related the startling story to her husband, who was wholly incredulous. But she herself had not the slightest doubt that she had seen and conversed with her recently departed mother. We can easily imagine the impatience with which she awaited the coming of morning, and with which she hurried to her mother's late residence at the earliest possible moment. As she approached the house her father and sister appeared on the veranda.

Now it seems that Mrs. Reeves Snyder had the reputation of being a dreamer of remarkable dreams, and her father, who was strongly inclined to conservatism, called out as she approached, "Have you had another dream?" To this she replied that she had dreamed of her mother. He interrupted her with the remark that her sister also had dreamed of her mother, and added that before her sister spoke of it at all he wished to hear her full story. It was related to him as above given, and then the amazed skeptic said that her sister had just told him of her own dream, which was identical in every detail. She had also dreamed that her dead mother came to her during the night, recounting the same story of the lost bonds, with the same minute instructions for recovering them. Together the three made their way to the place designated and there, in an empty tin can covered with a board, lay the missing bonds!

It requires no argument to show that the explanation of these facts is utterly beyond the possibilities of the materialistic hypothesis. But if it be true, as set forth in the hypothesis stated in Chapter I, that sleep and death differ only in that one is temporary and the other permanent release from the physical body, and that in each case the consciousness is then functioning through a vehicle of astral matter, then communication between the "dead" and the living is a perfectly natural thing during the hours of sleep. With some people this memory of the meeting may be vivid and realistic. With others it may be vague, unsubstantial and fleeting. With still others there may be no memory at all impressed upon the physical brain, yet the experience may have been as impressive to the person's consciousness at the moment as in the case of the others who did remember upon awakening.

In what other possible way can the facts be explained? The only person who knew where the bonds rested had been dead some weeks. No other person even knew that the bonds had been removed from their accustomed place of security. They were in a place where nobody would have thought for a moment of searching for them. They would have been safe from the most painstaking burglar. It required definite instruction to find them. How did that detailed information get into the consciousness of the two sisters, sleeping in different houses, at the same time? Another dream of discovery presents precisely the same principles but differs most interestingly in its details. The facts were given to me by Dr. L. H. Henley, who was at the time, and still is, chief surgeon of the Texas and Pacific Railway hospital at Marshall, Texas. His friends, a Mr. and Mrs. Moore, lived on a farm four and a half miles from Atlanta, Texas, at the time of the financial panic of 1907. Mr. Moore had deposited to his account at his bank about five thousand dollars. It will be remembered that during that brief financial stringency the banks were permitted to limit the amount that could be drawn out by depositors and that for some time only a small percentage of any balance could be checked out within a stated period. This experience of being unable to get his money when he wanted it seems to have raised a question in the mind of Mr. Moore about the wisdom of patronizing banks at all, and he evidently resolved that as soon as the restrictions had been removed he would withdraw his money and put it in a safe place. Just what happened between the resumption by the banks of the customary rules of procedure and the unexpected death of Mr. Moore soon afterward, nobody knows. But when his wife went to the bank, in closing up the estate, expecting to find about five thousand dollars to the credit of her late husband, she was astounded when informed that he had withdrawn the entire sum and closed the account. Now that five thousand dollars was the total of their little fortune and she faced grim poverty alone. She was obliged to abandon the home and go to live with a married daughter at Texarkana. More than two years passed. She supposed that her husband had invested or deposited the money somewhere, and neglected to mention the matter to her, and she could only vaguely hope that it would sometime in some way be brought to her attention and that she would at last learn the truth.

She finally did learn the truth- the strange and improbable truth- and in a most astounding manner. She dreamed one night that she was with her husband and that he told her the secret of the missing money. He had said to her in the dream that he drew the money from the bank in gold and silver coin and that on a day when nobody but himself was at home he had buried the treasure full three feet below the surface of the ground, on a line running from a certain corner of the house to a certain corner of a shed, and exactly midway between the two points.

So vivid and realistic was the dream that Mrs. Moore had absolute confidence that it presented the facts; but when she related it to her daughter's husband and asked him for the money necessary to make the journey to the village of Atlanta he ridiculed the whole thing so mercilessly that Mrs. Moore began to lose her confidence. But again she dreamed of it and again her husband showed her the exact spot of the buried coin, urging her to recover it. The repetition of the dream, however, did not move the skeptic. He declined to furnish money for such an apparently absurd investment. But again and again the dream recurred and Mrs. Moore could no longer endure the suspense. Concealing the purpose of the loan she casually asked her son-in-law to lend her five dollars, which he readily did. She hurried to the station and purchased a ticket for Atlanta. Alighting at the village she was fortunate enough to find the old negro who had been employed on the farm. He obtained a spade and they drove out to the old home. Carefully measuring the distance according to the dream directions the exact spot where the money was alleged to be secreted was ascertained and the negro began to dig. In due time he unearthed the carefully protected coin, three feet below the surface. Mrs. Moore returned in triumph with nearly five thousand dollars.

In this interesting case with its happy denouement the question naturally arises, "If this dream really represented a meeting of the consciousness of the dead husband and that of the living wife, why did he delay so long about giving the information?" The answer is that by the hypothesis the delay was not in giving the information but was probably caused by the inability of Mrs. Moore to impress it upon her physical brain and thereby bring it through into her waking consciousness. Apparently only after long continued effort did she finally triumph; but once she had succeeded in bringing the memory through into the waking state she was able to repeat it any number of times.

Another case of treasure recovered presents quite different circumstances. At the time of the discovery of the gold the old miser who had buried it had been dead more than seventy years and there was nothing that we know of to cause the dreamer to be thinking of him, or of a hidden fortune. The story was printed January 21, 1908, by the New York World, whose reporter went very fully into the details: "'Miss Lucy Alvord of Taylortown, N. L, told her brother Claude on Sunday morning that her grandfather, who died in 1837, came to her in a dream the night before, appearing so natural that, although she had never seen a picture of him. she recognized him from her mother's description. Pie was middle-aged and wore a beard. In the dream he seemed to shake Miss Alvord and arouse her. She stared at him and was about to speak, but he indicated silence and motioned her to follow him. She followed him into the kitchen of the house, a wing that was built long before the Revolution. The house itself has been occupied by the Alvord family for five generations.

Stepping to the north side of the great room the man opened the iron door or the brick oven alongside the fireplace. He stepped inside the big oven and reappeared with a stone jar which he set on the table in the middle of the room. He then seemed oblivious to the presence of Miss Alvord, and to her, in the dream, his conduct seemed perfectly natural. He dug his hands into the crock and brought them out filled with gold pieces. He emptied the crock on the table and began to stack and count the money. He made separate stacks of English and American coins and of the different denominations. He made figures on a slip of paper, which he totaled and put in his pocket.

"Then the visitor put the money back into the crock and crawled into the oven. Miss Alvord peered in and saw him wall up the crock with bricks and mortar. The oven is six feet deep and the wall was scarcely noticeable in the great depth. When all had been secured the man closed and locked the iron door. Then Miss Alvord woke up. When she met her brother at breakfast she told him the story. The vividness of her dream had frightened her. But she insisted that her brother attack the wall of the oven. She was confident that he would find the stone crock and the treasure. He laughed at her, but to humor her went at the wall with a crowbar. The first light blow went through the wall. A few blows demolished it, and there lay a crock such as the woman had seen in her dream. The excitement of the sister and brother knew no bounds. They dragged out the crock and opened it, and before their eyes lay gold. They emptied it on the kitchen table- a table made generations ago out of a slab of pine. They counted the money. In the heap of gold was four thousand and some odd dollars. The hoard belonged to Silas Alvord, the grandfather, in all probability. He was the last of the family to work an iron forge on the place. He made anchors, anchor chains and other implements. When he died, in 1837, it was thought he had a fortune. Apparently, however, he left nothing but the farm, valuable in itself. Then his relatives thought he had lost his money in wildcat banks. Miss Alvord's story of the strange dream and of the finding of the hoard of gold was told about the countryside, and all day yesterday neighbors heard her repeat it and looked in the oven and saw where the bricks had been removed."

Still another dream of discovery, resulting in the recovery of several thousand dollars in gold coin, is reported from Lancaster, Pennsylvania, which indicates that while the physical body is asleep the consciousness escapes its material confinement, and may bring back to the waking hours information which it has acquired in the ethereal regions. The following story appeared in the Associated Press dispatches sent out from Lancaster June 19, 1916 and was widely reprinted throughout the country:

"When John Bellman, farmer, near Brickerville, died six months ago, very little money was found, though the widow knew he had a substantial amount. In April, William Heil took possession of the farm, and he, too, made fruitless searches for Bellman's money. Tuesday night he dreamed that Bellman came to his bedside and told him that the money was buried in the hay-mow. Yesterday morning he and his wife searched in that place and found a box, deep hidden in the hay, and upon opening it, found thousands of dollars in five, ten and twenty dollar gold pieces. The widow of Bellman was notified, and took possession of the wealth. Those interested will not tell the amount, but reports have it from $5,000 to $15,000."

On September 25, 1909, the New York Evening Journal published this: "More than five years ago Myra Auld, the half grown daughter of S. M. Auld, living near New Wilmington, Pennsylvania, dreamed that on the farm next to that on which her father lived there had been buried a pot of gold. She induced her father to buy this farm when opportunity offered, and since that time she has been searching for the gold which she saw in her dreams. Today her perseverance was rewarded when she brought up from the bottom of an old, abandoned well on the farm $8,000 in gold, which had been buried for evidently twenty years. The farm had been owned by James Buchanan, a rather eccentric farmer, who died some years since. He had the reputation of being a miser and was always in great fear of robbers. Some years before his death Buchanan told some of his neighbors that he had buried some gold where those who did not deserve it would not find it. It had evidently been the intention of Buchanan to make some mention of this in a will which he intended to have written before his death, but he died suddenly, and the will which he had made some years before stood. The gold money was in an old powder can and it was filled level full with the gold, and the lid had been roughly soldered on and the whole affair wrapped in an old gunny sack. Miss Auld declares that she had searched every square foot of the farm at least twenty different times in the last five years, and that this was her tenth trip into the old well. Some animal had burrowed in the earth by the can and had exposed part of the old sack which enwrapped the can of gold. William Hays, administrator of the Buchanan estate, admits the finding of the gold and says he will lay claim to it in the name of the estate."

This case is not so strong as the preceding ones, but it is worthy a place in the ever-growing catalog of facts which reveal the real nature of human consciousness. In this case the miser had told some of his neighbors that he had buried the gold, presumably on his farm, and the skeptical will argue that the girl had heard these stories and, believing them, had induced her father to purchase the farm. This is possible and it reduces the value of the evidence to the testimony of Miss Auld. That should be given the same weight that it would have in any other matter. She asserts that she saw the gold in her dreams, but evidently could not definitely locate it, and says that because of her dreams she induced her father to secure the farm. There seems to be no possible motive for telling the dream story unless it is true. There was nothing to be gained by it. If the tales told by neighbors, of the miser's hidden gold, led to the purchase of the farm there appears to be no conceivable reason for fabricating the dream story.

But the case lacks the strength of the preceding ones, in which the sequel furnishes overwhelming evidence and leaves us with no possible alternative conclusion. A case in which a dream was the means of recovering the body of a lost son is given in the New York American, of October 18, 1915, under the title "Mother's Dream Saves Son From Potter's Field."

The story follows:

"A mother's graphic dream in which she saw the body of her long missing son being lowered into a pauper's grave has led to the discovery of the body. It marks one of the strangest incidents in local police history. Harry Kauffman, of No. 264 Cherry Street, disappeared June 30. His body was found July 4 and buried the same day among unidentified dead. The only record aside from mere description was that death had been due to drowning. Last week Mrs. Liba Kauffman dreamed all the details of the recovery and burial of her son's body. She informed her husband. He went to the Bureau of Unidentified Dead. The details as made known to his wife in the dream tallied in essentials with the actual incidents connected with the burial of Kauffman's body. It was soon learned that the body buried on July 4 really was that of the missing boy. Orders were then given to have it exhumed. Yesterday the funeral was held from the Kauffman home."

DREAMS AND PREMONITIONS

In this case about three months pass and the mother, who no doubt had been thinking daily of her son and mourning for him, at last brings the knowledge of the facts into her waking consciousness. Many another mother may have had a similar experience, and may have longed as earnestly for a clue to the mysterious disappearance of her boy, and yet failed to get it. One of the world's greatest psychologists, who enjoys the advantage of highly developed clairvoyance to facilitate his studies, remarks that there is nothing strange about the fact that a very small percentage of astral experiences are brought through into the waking state, but that the greater wonder is that anything at all is brought through on account of the fact that in order to do so there must be the rare combination of astral, mental and physical conditions that make it possible. The factors involved are, naturally enough, many and varied but the degree of sensitiveness represented by the dreamer is certainly a most important one.

Among dreams of discovery one of the most dramatic is that connected with the Wilkins case at San Francisco in 1908. When the mystery of the missing woman could not be explained and, when, with Wilkins in their hands, the officers of the law could get no tangible evidence to support the well-grounded suspicion that he had killed his wife, a neighbor came forward with a dream clue. Mrs. Wilkins had long before disappeared and her husband had given contradictory and improbable explanations of her prolonged "visit in the east." But absence and suspicion are not evidence and there was an embarrassing halt in the proceedings. Wilkins would undoubtedly have been liberated on account of the lack of evidence had not Mrs. Anderson urged the authorities to begin excavations in the barn. She declared that in repeated dreams she had seen the missing woman walk slowly to the barn, where an open grave was pointed out. The suggestion of the dreamer was finally reluctantly acted upon and the dead body was discovered and exhumed.

DREAMS AND PREMONITIONS

A more recent case in which a dream led to the discovery of a crime is reported by the Spokesman Review, Spokane, Washington, of May 23, 1916. The story follows:

"After a dream in which he saw his son, Dallas Greene, who had been missing for nearly a month, killed by a man, J. W. Greene, of W. 1002 Seventh Avenue, visited Troy, Mont., Saturday, and after a search with officers found his son's body buried in a dense thicket of brush on Callahan creek, about a mile from town. The circumstances indicated that murder had been committed, and Jack Miller, with whom Greene is said to have been camped near the spot of the supposed murder, and who is alleged to have sold horses which formerly belonged to Greene, was placed under arrest and now is in the jail at Libby."

On July 18, the Missoula Sentinel published a dispatch from Libby, Montana, giving the following additional information:

"John C. Miller, arrested for the murder of Dallas A. Greene, was brought before a jury in the district court yesterday for trial. The discovery of the murder came about when W. J. Greene, father of the dead man, dreamed he saw his son being killed. Frightened by the dream, the father came to this place from Spokane, leading the Sheriff to the spot where the body was concealed. Miller was arrested while trying to sell the deceased's live stock. He told friends that Greene had given him the horses to settle up an old debt."

Whether it transpires that Dallas Greene was murdered by Miller, or not, the value of the dream remains unchanged. Somebody killed Greene and hid the body in the thicket. The young man's father dreamed that his son had been murdered and was sufficiently impressed by the dream to begin the search immediately. A case in which it required repeated efforts to attain success is related by the Denver Post, of October 24, 1915. This

DREAMS AND PREMONITIONS

is the story:

"A woman's faith in a dream and her adherence to injunctions given there by her father may be the means of winning a $14,233 law suit for that father's former partner and of saving the partner from a jail judgment. On successive nights last week Mrs. Carl F. Vote, 2531 Stout Street, dreamed that her father, Charles F. Leimer, came to talk to her. Mr. Leimer died a year ago. The first two dreams were identical. In each she told her father exactly how she had disposed of her property since he had died, and asked his advice. The father attempted to tell her what to do- and she woke up. The third night she dreamed the same, but did not wake up. Her father advised her as to the care of the property, and further told her to look in an old trunk in the attic for some papers. These he told her to take to his former partner, Sylvester Knuttel, a real estate man. The next morning she had almost decided not to heed the admonition, for she had gone through the trunk many times before and was sure that nothing worth while had been left there. But she was convinced from the three dreams that the spirit of her father was trying to communicate something of importance. She looked, found the papers, but did not realize their significance until she took them to Knuttel. He was overjoyed to receive them, and told her they would prove conclusively his title to eight lots in Berkeley and some land in Jefferson county, which are the basis of a suit by Mrs. Eva May Strong for $14,233. Leimer, he said, had been taking care of the papers for him, and at his death they were lost. Mrs. Strong, who is the daughter-in-law of the late millionaire, Samuel Strong, is suing for title to the lots and for heavy punitive damages from Knuttel, also demanding that Knuttel be sent to jail until any judgment returned against him is satisfied."

This is a case in which there was certainly good reason for making strenuous and sustained effort to impress upon the mind of the dreamer the whereabouts of the missing papers.

DREAMS AND PREMONITIONS

What can the materialistic hypothesis possibly do with the facts presented in these dreams of discovery? Before the testimony of these witnesses the adherents of that outgrown hypothesis stand silent. They can neither deny the facts nor explain them.

A recent writer on the mystery of dreams remarks that "dreams locating lost articles may be but drafts on the marvelous storehouse of subconscious memory." That would at least be a possible explanation where one loses a pocketknife or a key, searches in vain for the lost article, and then dreams of its exact location. But how can it explain the finding of things which the dreamer did not lose, of which there can be, neither consciously nor subconsciously, a memory record, and of which the dreamer knows nothing whatever beyond what he learns from the dream state? In at least two of these cases (Reeves Snyder and Moore) information unknown to any living being is obtained during the hours of sleep, is immediately put to the test, and results in the recovery of valuables.

In these two cases alone we have evidence of the soundness of the hypothesis laid down in Chapter I, which is not merely convincing in its character but is also conclusive in its facts.

CHAPTER IV

Varieties of Dreams

While many dreams may be traced to material causes there are many others which undoubtedly owe their origin to the activities of the ethereal world where, functioning in his astral body while the physical body sleeps, the dreamer is more or less awake to, and conscious of, what is going on about him.

To people who have thought but little upon such subjects there will, at first, be no apparent difference between a dream which results from the automatic action of the idle physical brain and its etheric counterpart, and the dream which is the result of astral activities, recalled at the moment of awakening. Each is but a memory, a mental picture associated with various emotions. But there is nevertheless a distinction and although it is often slight and elusive at first it grows to definiteness with experience. Upon first entering a garden filled with a profusion of blossoms it is difficult to distinguish between the various delicate perfumes but after a little experience one is able to separate and recognize the different odors. And somewhat thus it is in the subtle regions of the dream. What is at first elusive becomes definite and unmistakable with experience.

Every dreamer is aware that there are, broadly speaking, two general classes of memories which he calls dreams. In one the dream is more or less chaotic, disjointed, illogical and fantastic. Such dreams are usually the result of the automatic action of the brain. They lack coherence and logic because the thinker, the ego, is not there. He has withdrawn his consciousness with the separation of the astral body from the physical body and is either dreamily drifting about in his astral vehicle or is alert to his surroundings, according to his stage of evolution. The physical body has temporarily lost its tenant as certainly as a suit of clothes abandoned before retiring has lost its occupant. When the ego returns to it's tenement of clay and the center of consciousness is transferred once more to the physical brain, the fragmentary brain pictures become a part of the memory.

These more or less fantastic thought images sometimes owe their origin in part to external stimuli, and the brain, without the directing intelligence of the ego, may magnify the pressure of a button into the stab of a dagger, or the sound of a rolling marble into the roar of artillery. In such dreams the most ludicrous situations cause no mirth and the most impossible transactions call out no challenge from the reason, because no intellect is present to protest against the riot of chaos. There is a total absence of relationship between cause and effect, while all laws of space and matter, have disappeared. The dreamer is at one moment walking through the quiet country lanes near his home and the next instant may be seated on the throne of Siam. He changes personality with equal facility and may become, in a twinkling, one of his neighbors or his own grandfather without the slightest suspicion that it is a rather remarkable transformation. He may pass swiftly from a pleasant chat with a friend to a furious quarrel in which his friend changes into a bandit and slays him; and, after calmly looking down on his own corpse for a moment he rises from the dead, drags his murderer into court and gives testimony about his own assassination without for a moment being aware that there is anything either illogical or impossible in the whole affair.

The other class of dreams differs from all this as intelligence differs from stupidity, or mental balance differs from insanity. This class of dreams consists of either the experiences of the man in the astral region while the abandoned physical body is asleep, or else of some truth of nature or some premonition which the ego attempts, with more or less success, to impress upon the physical brain and which is in some degree remembered upon awakening. Such dreams are akin to the activities of the waking consciousness in that they are orderly, coherent and logical. Different people will recall the events with varying degrees of success, some being able to remember only a very little while others review all the details with as vivid recollection as the occurrences of yesterday's waking hours. But, whether the memory grasps little or much, all that is recalled will be reasonable and natural. The dreamer remembers that he has been to some place, which may or may not be a place that he knows in his waking consciousness; or he may remember that he has visited some friend, whether dead or living matters not, for when his living friend is asleep, he, also, is functioning in his astral body. The dreamer on awakening may sometimes have a memory of a conversation with somebody and, if so, it will be a sane and logical conversation, quite as able, or perhaps abler, than anything he is capable of in his waking state; for in the astral realm the center of his consciousness is nearer the ego and the thought is therefore a fuller and freer expression of himself than it is when expressed through the physical brain. This fact explains why occasionally some great poem is written, or invention is made, or problem is solved, by thought brought through into the waking consciousness from the sleeping hours.

It not infrequently happens that one who has recently lost a very dear companion or friend remembers upon awakening to have been with him. If the memory is vivid and the event seems realistic there is very strong probability that the dream is the memory of an astral experience. Quite often the dreamer will bring back a memory of the emotions aroused by renewed association with the departed- a lingering memory of joy and exaltation. Such memories from the ethereal world are, with some people, full and complete, while with others they are the merest fragments. As a rule they come at widely separated periods, and months may elapse between them. This is not in the least because the association is not renewed night after night, for it invariably is, but wholly because the dreamer is unable to impress the memory of it upon the brain consciousness. It is possible to cultivate the ability to do so and slowly but steadily to expand the consciousness until one is enabled to bring a full and vivid memory of the astral activities into the daily life; but a full discussion of the details essential to success in the undertaking can best be left for a following chapter.

The dreams that are the result of the automatic activity of the physical brain or of vagrant vibrations drifting through its etheric counterpart, may be dismissed as being of no importance whatever. It is necessary to classify them only to eliminate them. The dreams that are memories of the hours spent in the ethereal regions may be extremely important to one who will take the trouble to understand them because they are the activities of his consciousness working on higher levels. That higher state of consciousness is so radically different from its expression conditioned by physical matter that it is impossible to comprehend it fully, but the fragments of it that come through into the waking state at least prove its almost omniscient character.

Having eliminated the dreams arising from physical causes we may now classify the remainder. These may be divided into two classes and be designated as dreams that are the memories of astral experiences and dreams that are the result of the attempt of the ego to impress ideas or facts upon the brain consciousness. Dreams of the latter variety are often symbolical for, as has been well said, symbology is the language of the soul. Obviously, facts or ideas impressed on the brain consciousness by the ego himself are likely to be of the greatest importance. The ideas may represent profound truths of nature and the facts may disclose the future or contain a warning that it may be extremely desirable to fully comprehend. The success of the ego's attempt, however, necessarily depends upon a number of things and a little thought on the subject will suffice to show why failure is common. C. W. Leadbeater, in his valuable little volume, Dreams, says:

"A result which follows from the ego's supernormal method of time-measurement is that in some degree prevision is possible to him. The present, the past, and, to a certain extent, the future lie open before him if he knows how to read them; and he undoubtedly thus foresees at times events that will be of interest or importance to his lower personality, and makes more or less successful endeavors to impress them upon it. When we take into account the stupendous difficulties in his way in the case of an ordinary person- the fact that he is himself probably not yet even half awake, that he has hardly any control over his various vehicles, and cannot, therefore, prevent his message from being distorted or altogether overpowered by the surgings of desire, by the casual thought-currents in the etheric part of his brain, or by some slight physical disturbance affecting his denser body- we shall not wonder that he so rarely fully succeeds in his attempt. Once, now and again, a complete and perfect forecast of some event is vividly brought back from the realms of sleep; far more often the picture is distorted or unrecognizable, while sometimes all that comes through is a vague sense of some impending misfortune, and still more frequently nothing at all penetrates the denser body.

"It has sometimes been argued that when this prevision occurs it must be mere coincidence, since if events could really be foreseen they must be foreordained, in which case there can be no free-will for man. Man, however, undoubtedly does possess freewill; and therefore, as remarked above, prevision is possible only to a certain extent. In the affairs of the average man it is probably possible to a very large extent, since he has developed no will of his own worth speaking of, and is consequently very largely the creature of circumstances; his karma places him amid certain surroundings, and their action upon him is so much the most important factor in his history that his future course may be foreseen with almost mathematical certainty.

"When we consider the vast number of events which can be but little affected by human action, and also the complex and wide-spreading relation of causes to their effects, it will scarcely seem wonderful to us that on the plane where the result of all causes at present in action is visible, a very large portion of the future may be foretold with considerable accuracy even as to detail. That this can be done has been proved again and again, not only by prophetic dreams, but by the second-sight of the Highlanders and the predictions of clairvoyants; and it is on this forecasting of effects from the causes already in existence that the whole scheme of astrology is based. But when we come to deal with a developed individual- a man with knowledge and will- then prophecy fails us, for he is no longer the creature of circumstances, but to a great extent their master. True, the main events of his life are arranged beforehand by his past karma; but the way in which he will allow them to affect him, the method by which he will deal with them, and perhaps triumph over them- these are his own, and they cannot be foreseen except as probabilities. Such actions of his in their turn become causes, and thus chains of effects are produced in his life which were not provided for by the original arrangement, and, therefore, could not have been foretold with any exactitude."

It is not easy to comprehend in the physical brain consciousness how events can be known before they occur. May not the explanation be that they have occurred so far as inner planes are concerned, but that only as they work outward from the realm of causation and become materialized in what we call an event, can the limited physical consciousness become aware of them? If physical matter is a limitation of consciousness it must necessarily give rise to illusory ideas of the superphysical realms, where what we call past, present and future may represent entirely different conditions than we are now able to conceive. Sir Oliver Lodge says: "A luminous and helpful idea is that time is but a relative mode of regarding things; we progress through phenomena at a certain definite pace, and this subjective advance we interpret in an objective manner, as if events moved necessarily in this order and at this rate. But that may be only one mode of regarding them. The events may be in some sense in existence always, both past and future, and it may be we who are arriving at them, not they which are happening."

Whether or not we are able to harmonize our conceptions of the matter with the evidence of our senses, the evidence still remains. "However strange may be the phenomenon of precognition," says Professor Charles Richet, "we must not let ourselves be diverted from the truth by the strangeness of appearances. A fact is a fact, even though it may upset our conception of the universe; for our conception of the universe is terribly infantile."

It is scarcely possible to overemphasize the importance of the fact that people who have premonitory dreams represent a very wide range of mental and physical conditions and that in the impressions made upon the waking consciousness we must naturally expect corresponding complexity. Some people are prone to assert that since they have had dreams which have accurately forecast the future all their succeeding dreams should prove equally reliable and should be regarded as infallible authority. But this by no means follows. Until one has reached that advanced point in his evolution where the ego is in control of his vehicles of consciousness, and the physical and astral bodies have become fairly obedient to the will, it is idle to talk of the infallibility of such psychic impressions. It should be remembered that with the average person the memories of both astral experiences and egoic impressions are, at best, fragmentary. They are limited and very partial expressions of the higher consciousness. Such dreams, therefore, are not something which, even with fuller understanding and further development, can be used for our guidance in the affairs of daily life. They are fragmentary and partial, their expression is not within the control of the will, and they may at any time be distorted by the physical brain conditions of the moment and thus be rendered fantastic or ambiguous. This being true we cannot positively know the truth or falsity of such premonitions until the event they refer to has occurred.

In one instance the event transpires in perfect conformity to the dream while in another we find, perhaps, that what we expected to happen to ourselves really befalls a friend, or does not happen to anybody, so far as our physical plane knowledge goes. The reason for the failure of the premonition may be found in one of the foregoing explanations, or in still other possibilities as, for example, the fact that the waking consciousness has brought through only a part of the entire drama, dropping out vital factors that would have modified or set aside that which we remember, and thus we have mistaken a fragment for the whole.

But regardless of the fact that we cannot always use such flashes from the ego to shape a course in daily life, they are none the less useful and valuable in revealing the true nature of our consciousness; and although we cannot harness them to rules and exceptions they occasionally play an important and beneficent part in our lives. Furthermore, by carefully studying them we can arrive finally at a point where we can rely upon them because we shall thus have hastened the arrival of that period in our evolution where the waking and sleeping hours are united in unbroken consciousness; where the distorting factors in brain transmission will have disappeared and the unshadowed wisdom of the ego will come freely through into the physical life.

CHAPTER V

Premonitory Dreams

The ego is the source of most premonitions. The dream may be a warning to one's self or may be intended for another; or it may convey some information about the future. It may be vivid in detail or it may merely leave a very vague impression of impending events. But whatever its character and degree of efficiency it is usually the result of the effort of the ego to convey important information to the waking consciousness. Premonitory dreams are comparatively rare. They usually relate to some very important matter that is not far ahead in the physical life of the dreamer, or some one closely associated with him; and as such events are not numerous the premonitions are correspondingly few. Naturally enough, accidents and death are the subjects with which premonitions frequently deal.

There have been many notable examples and one which will come instantly to mind is Abraham Lincoln's premonition of approaching death. We have very definite information on the subject and know that he spoke to his bodyguard of the matter the evening before the assassination, and made some philosophical remarks about death. It is said that he interrupted the last cabinet meeting he ever held to speak of a dream and Gideon Welles, Lincoln's secretary of the navy, wrote down the details in his diary. Lincoln was a great dreamer and appears to have attached much importance to what he dreamed. In a series of articles entitled Lincoln and Booth, by Winfield M. Thompson, which were widely published by a newspaper syndicate in 1915, Mr. Thompson writes as follows of Lincoln's last dreams:

"A few days before his death Lincoln related to his wife and a few friends the story of a strange dream that had disturbed

51

him the night before. In his dream, he said, he went from room to room in the White House, and everywhere heard sounds of pitiful sobbing though no living being was in sight, until I arrived at the east room. Before me was a catafalque, on which rested a corpse. Around it were stationed soldiers. There was a throng of people, some gazing sorrowfully upon the corpse whose face was covered, others weeping pitifully. 'Who is dead in the White House?' I demanded of one of the soldiers. 'The President' was his answer. 'He was killed by an assassin.' Then came a loud burst of grief from the crowd, which woke me from my dream.'

On the afternoon of Friday, April 14, a few hours before he fell under the assassin's bullet, Lincoln held his last cabinet meeting. It was remarkable for two things- the depth of charity and love displayed by Lincoln in a discussion on the return to the Union of the seceded states and a curious vein of mysticism the President displayed in describing a premonitory dream he had had the night before. General Grant, who had just arrived from Appomattox, was invited to attend the meeting and did so. Grant was anxious about Sherman, who was confronted by the army of General Joseph E. Johnston in the vicinity of Goldsboro, N. C., and expressed a desire for news from him. The President responded by saying that he thought that all was well with Sherman- a dream had caused him to feel so. He then described the dream. His manner while doing so made a deep impression on most of the men about him."

Gideon Welles' diary gave in extended detail what was said about the dream which had reference to the approach of important events and which, Lincoln declared, did not herald success but merely indicated that something very important was approaching. The record by Secretary Welles runs thus:

"The president remarked that news would come soon and come favorably, he had no doubt, for he had last night his usual dream, which had preceded nearly every great event of the war. We inquired the particulars of this remarkable dream. He said it was in my element- it related to the water; that he seemed to be in a singular and indescribable vessel, but always the same, and that he was moving with great rapidity toward a dark and indefinite shore; that he had had this same singular dream preceding the firing on Sumter and battles of Bull Run, Antietam, Gettysburg, Stone River, Vicksburg, Wilmington, etc. General Grant remarked with some emphasis and asperity that Stone River was no victory- that a few such victories would have ruined the country and that he knew of no important results from it. The President said that perhaps he should not altogether agree with him but whatever might be the facts, his singular dream preceded that fight. Victory did not always follow his dream but the event and results were important. He had no doubt that a battle had taken place or was about to be fought 'and Johnston will be beaten; for I had this strange dream again last night. It must relate to Sherman; my thoughts are in that direction and I know of no other very important event which is likely just now to occur."

On March 13, 1915, Col. W. H. Crook, disbursing officer of the White House, died at an advanced age, after fifty years of continuous government service. It was early in 1865 that he became Lincoln's bodyguard. His passing revived the stories he used to tell of his association with the great statesman and among those that appeared with the announcement of his death was this testimony about the dream that foretold the President's death:

"Col. Crook told often of how, on the afternoon before Lincoln's assassination, the President had come to him in confidence and said that on successive nights he had dreams which foretold his murder. Crook thereupon begged the President not to go to the theater that evening as planned. Lincoln insisted, and furthermore would not hear of Crook accompanying him. He ordered Crook to go home and rest."

An interesting case of premonition of approaching death is that of Dr. I. F. Bacon, of San Francisco, who was killed in the earthquake of 1906. He was not able to bring into his waking consciousness any of the details but he had been sufficiently impressed with the truth of the approaching calamity to have an unchangeable conviction that death was just ahead. The following account appeared in the San Francisco Examiner, May 3, 1906:

"For two days before the earthquake Dr. J. F. Bacon was haunted by a premonition of sudden death. He was killed by the collapse of the house in which he lived. Dr. Bacon was well known in San Francisco. He was a prominent practitioner, and also the proprietor of a drug store at 303 Folsom St. Several times during the day immediately preceding the disaster he mentioned his fears to his friends. Instinctively he felt that a terrible fate was impending for him, and while he had no idea what was the nature of the threatened accident, he declared that it would kill him. To A. W. Vance, a real estate dealer, who was graduated from College in Dr. Bacon's class, he spoke of the morbid idea which possessed him. 'I can't tell what it is,' he said, 'but I know that I will meet a sudden death within a day or two. It is impossible to explain.' When the tremblor struck San Francisco the house in which Dr. Bacon was sleeping at Sixth and Folsom, fell to the ground, burying him in the debris. Deceased was a graduate of the class of 1876 of the Medical College of the Pacific."

Two years later another prominent citizen of San Francisco died suddenly after a premonition of the approaching close of physical life. From the Berkeley Gazette of August 25, 1908, the following account is taken:

"When Eugene Grace, once a leader in the Southern

colony and prominent in San Francisco business circles, dropped dead while running to catch a train in Berkeley Monday evening, it was but the working out of a premonition of death he had received twenty four hours before. So strongly was he influenced by this innate knowledge of his approaching end that he had made a final disposition of his effects and requested that his body be shipped to his sister in Atlanta, Georgia. It was in the Regent Hotel, 562 Sutter Street, San Francisco, where he lived, that he received the inkling of death in the near future. He disposed of his property and asked John F. Shea to ship his body south. He spoke of his affairs, saying that what remained of a life insurance policy of a thousand dollars, after the funeral expenses had been deducted, should be given to his nephew and namesake in Atlanta. Then, having done all that was necessary on this earth, he bravely thrust away the subject of death. At one time Grace was a leading figure in San Francisco. Courtly, chivalrous, kindhearted, a typical southern gentleman, he was immensely popular everywhere."

In studying the phenomena of premonitions the question naturally arises, "Why does the ego impress, or try to impress, a warning upon the waking consciousness?" The reason appears to be plain enough. When a physician knows that death must soon come to his patient he discloses the truth to him. He never permits death to come suddenly and unexpectedly upon him if he can prevent it, but gives him time to arrange his affairs and "put his house in order." From the purely physical viewpoint there is excellent reason for this course.

If death is inevitable it is clearly much better to know it a short time in advance. (To be advised of the fact too far in advance of the event would obviously not be an advantage.) So even if death is unavoidable the premonition is of great value. But deaths or accidents which are the subjects of premonitions sometimes are avoidable and have been thus escaped. When we remember the difficulties with which the ego must deal in impressing the lower mind with such warnings it is easy to understand how very partial and insufficient most of them must be to the brain consciousness. A premonition that is intended to be full and vivid in detail may register in the brain merely as a vague impression of impending danger, or perhaps as an unshakable conviction of approaching death, as in the case of Dr. Bacon, but be utterly lacking in details that can lead to a course of action.

In the case of Eugene B. Grace, above mentioned, who can say that death might not have been avoided if he had known just where the danger lay? Had Dr. Bacon known that an earthquake would raze the building in which he was accustomed to sleep, would he have left the city the day before it occurred? To what extent accident and death might be avoided if the people who have premonitions were more sensitive, would be a difficult guess. Cases are not wanting in which the ego appears, by repeated and prolonged efforts, to be endeavoring to impress the danger of a situation upon the brain so firmly that it will be realized in the waking hours. This seems to have been the case with Thomas W. Ewing, of Pueblo, Colorado, a locomotive engineer employed on the Denver and Rio Grande railway, in 1908. Mr. Ewing's run was westward from Pueblo.

For several successive nights he dreamed of a terrible accident in which he seemed to be killed. So vivid and realistic were these dreams that he could not go to sleep again after awakening on account of the nervous condition they caused. He discussed the matter with his wife but, not believing in premonitions, they decided that overwork or some unknown nerve disorder must be responsible for the remarkable dreams. On the day following the last of the dreams, while his locomotive was standing on a siding at Florence, Colorado, the boiler exploded, instantly killing both Ewing and his fireman. Had the ego been endeavoring to impress upon the lower mind in this case the fact that the locomotive was in dangerous condition and picturing the consequences that must soon follow if they were not avoided? It seems rather remarkable that a dream repeated so persistently and impressively should have been ignored even if details were not brought through into waking consciousness.

A case in which the premonition did serve the purpose is that of Mrs. Hugh Larue, of Briceville, Tennessee. On December 9, 1911, occurred the disastrous explosion in the Cross Mountain coal mine. On the next day the New York Herald published the following account:

"After a terrific explosion, that shook the earth for a wide area, 207 men were entombed today in the Cross Mountain coal mine of the Knoxville Iron Company. Hugh Larue, a miner employed in the shaft, owes his life to a dream his wife had last night. When he arose this morning and prepared to go to his daily task Mrs. Larue refused to prepare his lunch for him to carry to the mines. She did not want him to work today. She then recited a dream she had. In her dream she saw scores of miners with their heads blown off being carried out of the mine entrance as she and her little children stood at the mine's mouth. Larue had not missed a day from his work for many months, but he was prevailed upon to remain out of the mines. It was only a short time after Mrs. Larue told her story that the explosion occurred."

A great disaster usually furnishes several examples of premonitions. Where several hundred people are concerned it may reasonably be expected that a few among them are sensitive enough to be impressed with the doom that awaits them. The Titanic disaster furnished several cases, each possessing more or less evidential value, dependent upon circumstances and upon whether or not the principals involved mentioned the facts to others prior to the sailing of the ship. Among the strong cases is that of the Hon. J. Cannon Middleton. The Titanic was scheduled to sail April 10. It appears from the evidence that Mr. Middleton purchased his ticket on March 23. A few days later he dreamed that the great steamer was wrecked and in the dream he saw her surrounded by passengers and crew swimming about her. When the dream recurred the following night he began to feel decidedly uneasy about it but said nothing, probably for fear of uselessly alarming his family. Fortunately for him a cablegram arrived six days before the ship sailed, suggesting a postponement of the journey on account of business conditions. Supplied now with what seemed to him a tangible reason he had his ticket canceled and then told his wife and several friends of the dreams. The books of the White Star company and the canceled ticket, which Mr. Middleton retains, furnish part of the evidence.

Nobody will deny that when there is an elaboration of details, coincidence is an impossible explanation. If a dream is vague in outline and lacking in detail, and later something occurs that corresponds in a general way with the dream, we may reasonably enough dismiss it as mere coincidence. One dreams, let us say, that a fortune is inherited and soon after a relative dies bequeathing property to the dreamer; or one dreams of being seriously injured and later has an arm broken in a railway wreck. While such dreams may, or may not, be actually connected with the succeeding events, coincidence is a possible explanation. But when the dream presents a wealth of details, and the following event corresponds exactly, then coincidence is an absurd and impossible explanation. It is coincidence that Mr. A., in Chicago, is telling an amusing story of a man whom he once saw under hypnotic influence, at the same time that Mr. B., in St. Louis, is making himself ludicrous in a series of hypnotic antics. But it is impossible that every word and gesture and facial expression of Mr. B. and the man of whom Mr. A. speaks can be identical.

Coincidence can explain the concurrence of two general events but never an identity of details. Now, it is impossible to deny that dreams sometimes forecast the, minutest details. An

acquaintance gives me the following personal experience but without permission to use her name:

"I rarely dream, but several weeks before my husband passed on I dreamed of his death. I seemed to be taken into our living room where the casket was placed and saw him surrounded by floral pieces bearing the customary cards. As my husband was a splendid type of physical strength and had never been ill, except for an occasional cold, the dream made little impression upon me. I had no confidence in the reality of any kind of dreams and, after casually mentioning it to an intimate friend, I thought no more about it. Some weeks later my husband contracted pneumonia and died suddenly. My dream came vividly before me then, for every floral piece, every card, and the arrangement of the room, was identical with the dream."

Every student of psychology is familiar with the fact that dreams are very commonly expressed in symbology. It is the method of the ego, apparently, and it is definitely expressive of the ideas to be impressed upon the lower mind. Attention has already been directed to the fact that the inner planes are nearer to reality than the physical life. This symbolical language of the soul illustrates the point. As symbols are to words, the higher consciousness is to the lower. A story that would require a thousand of our clumsy words for its presentation may be expressed very briefly by symbols. But it must not be supposed that because a dream is symbolical it is, therefore, an accurate description and presents the facts with invariable certainty. Its reliability depends, as with any dream, upon the clearness of the translation in the lower mind and the freedom from confusion with the vibrations of the dense brain and its etheric counterpart.

Sometimes people who are interested in the study of dreams ask if there is some code in symbology which, when understood, will enable one to comprehend a dream expressed in symbols. The fact seems to be that symbols convey different meanings to different people and that each person who dreams in that fashion attaches to the symbols a significance of his own. He has, however, not the least doubt about the meaning of any particular symbol, and probably for the reason that the ego impresses its special significance as everything else is impressed. One person associates success, or an "all's well" feeling, with the symbol of a flag; another with flowers; one knows that dark water signifies danger, while another sees an animal or a reptile as the symbol of impending danger or misfortune. Is it not probable that the ego uses, for expressing facts to the lower consciousness, the symbols which that particular person can best understand? If one has a fear of water that would be the line of least resistance in impressing the idea of coming calamity. Another may feel perfectly at ease when about, or in, the water but may be filled with apprehension at sight of a mouse or a spider.

In that case the symbol of water would convey no warning, and serve no purpose in arousing and steadying the personality against a coming shock, while the symbol of the animal or the insect would. Therefore the meaning of the symbol varies with the temperament and experience of the individual.

A good illustration of the symbolical dream, in which the ego is first endeavoring to warn and fortify the lower mind against approaching trouble and later to impress the encouraging fact that the danger has passed, is contained in three dreams related to me by Mrs. Robert K. Walton, of Nordhoff, California. In the early part of January, 1915, she dreamed that while with her husband a dangling black spider appeared and that both of them began to fight it. Mrs. Walton had not been in really good health for several years but at the time of the dream she was in her usual health except for a slight fever which was thought to be the result of a trifling indisposition.

Nothing was farther from her mind than the thought

that the fever indicated anything serious. In the dream she felt that the spider must be killed. Instead, however, it disappeared. The scene suddenly changed and she found herself in a new, clean room, such as spiders are not likely to inhabit, and she experienced a feeling of relief. But suddenly she became aware that instead of having left her when it disappeared, the loathsome insect was now beneath her clothing! This dream Mrs. Walton related to her husband in the morning. A few days passed and as the slight fever did not leave her a physician was called in. He announced at once that her condition was such that she must go to a hospital the following day. It proved to be the beginning of an illness which continued several months. She had not been long in the hospital when a large abscess formed and, in due course, was lanced. This, and her general condition, gave weeks of pain and marked a distinct stage in her long illness. The doctor and nurse cheered her up with hopeful talk and she was looking forward to early recovery when the second dream occurred.

It was now the latter part of May. Mrs. Walton dreamed that she was in a garret and that in passing out of the door she put her hand in a spider's web. An enormous, vicious looking spider ran up her wrist, filling her with a feeling of horror. She awoke gasping with terror. This dream was related to the nurse with the prediction that it portended great trouble. The nurse made light of the matter, as nurses always do. But a few days later the doctor gently announced to the patient that a capital operation was necessary. It followed, and for some weeks she was a pawn in the game played by life and death. Life finally won and she arose and went out into the world again. But meantime a third dream had cheered her with its forecast of the truth, and no doubt helped in her recovery, as the others had helped to fortify her against approaching trouble.

It was only two or three days after the operation that the third dream occurred. Mrs. Walton dreamed that she was sitting in an arbor talking with her surgeon, not her physician. The surgeon looked about him. Overhead was an enormous spider. He pulled it down and flung it into a fire where it was consumed by the flames. It was the operation, notwithstanding its great danger, that finally closed the chapter of suffering and now for the first time in fourteen years she is enjoying good health. This series of dreams is, I am inclined to think, one of the most interesting on record. A little careful study of its details will reveal to the student of dream lore a better understanding of the watchfulness of the ego over the personality, and will indicate the extent to which helpful impressions would be received by everybody if they were more sensitive to them.

While the more tragic things of life are usually the subjects of premonitions there are, of course, exceptions to the rule. Sometimes, when apparently the astro-physical conditions are most favorable, commonplace things may be impressed on the brain and be clearly retained in the waking memory. It may occasionally descend from the commonplace even to the trivial. But instances in which only the ordinary drama of life, and that at least devoid of tragedy for the dreamer himself, is outlined in its immediate future, are fairly common. A case of this kind occurred recently in an eastern city. In June, 1916, a lady residing near me received a letter from Robert Donovan, of Brooklyn, N. Y., describing a premonitory dream. Mr. Donovan has an intimate friend whose profession is teaching. His family consisted of his elderly parents and a sister. The sister did the housekeeping and looked after the parents during the absence of her brother, who went daily to his school.

He was expecting to be married in the near future and this was well known to his friends. One night in March, 1916, Mr. Donovan dreamed that he was in conversation with his friend, the teacher, who told him that he would be married on May 20. In his dream Mr. Donovan glanced at the calendar and, observing that May 20th came on Saturday remarked that it was an unusual day for a wedding. "Why don't you wait till the school term has closed?" he asked his friend. The teacher replied that he could not do so but if he gave any reason the dreamer could not remember it. In the morning he related his dream to his mother who laughed at its improbability. Two weeks later the teacher's sister fell dead, and a difficult situation presented itself. There was nobody to stay with the parents while the teacher was absent. In this emergency the date of the marriage was advanced and the teacher wrote Mr. Donovan that, as the result of the unexpected developments, and of his professional engagements, the wedding would take place on Saturday, May 20.

While the ego is undoubtedly responsible for most of the premonitory dreams there are apparently cases in which the forecast of the future may be communicated by some entity of the ethereal regions. There are also on record some cases which appear to indicate that when the ego is unable to impress the lower mind the information is indirectly conveyed through another person who can be impressed; and it would appear that this sometimes occurs when there is nothing more important to be revealed than an impending set of circumstances which may cause disappointment and great annoyance, the distress of which may be somewhat softened by the knowledge that it is inevitable.

Much has been written about dreams which have enabled students to find the solution of perplexing mathematical or other problems. Many stories are told of inventions, poems and musical compositions coming from the dream state and being written out immediately upon awakening. By our hypothesis the explanation may be either that the dreamer gets the ideas from his own less restricted consciousness in higher realms, or that he gets them from others whom he meets in the astral regions and, in either case, is fortunate enough to retain the memory when he awakens. Robert Louis Stevenson, who appears to have known very much about the occult, tells us in Travels and Essays that the most original of his stories were sketched or composed in dreams- that he not only thus got perfect plots but saw it all dramatized. The dream state was apparently his final resort when the waking consciousness could not supply the necessary material. He had long tried, he says, to write something on dual personality, but in vain. Then he dreamed the essentials of The Strange Case of Dr. Jekyll and Mr. Hyde. And this was only an incident in many years of similar work. Olalla was "given" to him, he asserts, "in bulk and detail." He says that he merely added the external scenery and that the moral itself, of the story, came in the dream.

In what degree the ego, with marvelous grasp of the verities of nature, might illuminate the lower mind, and to what extent premonitions would warn us and guide us if we were all highly sensitive, and responsive to the delicate vibrations sent down into the physical brain, it is impossible to guess. The evidence furnished by the many well authenticated cases of premonitory dreams certainly indicates that the ego is continually endeavoring to impress ideas and facts upon the lower mind, but usually with no very great success.

CHAPTER VI

Memories of Astral Experiences

Excluding the trivial and fantastic dreams- those which are automatically produced by the physical mechanism of consciousness- by far the larger part of the remainder are the memories of astral experiences. Premonitions and also the dream- if it may properly be called a dream- in which the lower mind is impressed with some truth of nature not previously understood, naturally constitute a very small proportion of dream activities. Dreams which are the memories of what one has seen and heard and said and done in the astral consciousness during the time when the physical body sleeps are greater in number because they represent the ordinary affairs of life. Such dreams may come to any person who has attained that point in human evolution where the mind and emotions are fairly well controlled. The conditions are then present that render a recollection of the astral experiences at least possible, but it must not be forgotten that there must be a necessary combination of physical, astral and mental relationships that permit the vibrations of the astral matter to register themselves in the physical brain. It therefore commonly happens to the person who has reached the stage where he is conscious and active in the astral real in at night that he only occasionally recalls the experiences through which he has passed. When he attains this stage of his evolution, however, he will seldom, if ever, experience the old order of confused dream due to the senseless automatic activity of the physical brain. On the contrary, he will very probably have no dream memories at all upon awakening in the morning, except upon the infrequent occasions when he brings through a recollection of the astral experiences.

The frequency of this increases as his evolution proceeds, and he ultimately remembers all the astral experiences-a gratifying result that can be greatly hastened by giving studious attention to the matter. If we put aside the effort from the material side to bring back the memory and consider the matter in its relationship to the average person, then we may say that in premonitions we have a class of dreams that represents the direct efforts of the ego to impress the lower mind, while in dreams that are the results of astral experiences we have the memories which float through simply because, so to speak, all the intervening gates happen to be open at the same instant.

As more and more facts about dreams are collected the hypothesis here invoked to explain them will become stronger. Occasionally somebody has a unique dream that throws new light on the true nature of the dream state. In his lecture on Shakespeare (p. 45), Robert G. Ingersoll relates the following dream:

"I once had a dream, and in this dream I was discussing a subject with another man. It occurred to me that I was dreaming, and I then said to myself: If this is a dream I am doing the talking for both sides- consequently I ought to know in advance what the other man is going to say. In my dream I tried the experiment. I then asked the other man a question, and before he answered made up my mind what the answer was to be. To my surprise the man did not say what I expected he would, and so great was my astonishment that I awoke."

What Col. Ingersoll remembered as a dream was probably an actual conversation. Had he been familiar with the idea that while the physical body sleeps the consciousness functions through a subtler body, he could not have been surprised at the actual conversation in which the other man furnished his own ideas as he would do in the physical body. His memory of the incident on awakening was evidently a confused blending of the astral experience and his physical ideas of what dreams are. In Chapter I the difference between sleep and death was discussed, and the freedom of the soul, or consciousness, in ethereal realms while the physical body sleeps was pointed out. Since the relationship of physical and astral matter is that of interpenetration, as in the case of a sponge surrounded by water which both envelops it and permeates it, passing into the astral region is not necessarily a journey in space.

But it may mean that, and may represent movement of the astral body that is extraordinarily rapid as compared with anything of which we know in the physical world. But however far afield one may journey in the astral body there remains a magnetic connection with the physical body. Clairvoyant investigations reveal the fact that in the case of people of low evolutionary development the astral body remains during sleep in the immediate vicinity of the physical body, while with the person of average mental and moral development it moves freely through the astral regions as the vehicle of his consciousness. The experiences gained naturally present great variety.

Mrs. Ella R. Tuttle, of Rochester, N. Y., furnishes two dreams in which the accuracy of the waking memory was promptly sustained by physical facts. In 1898 she dreamed that her mother, who was dead, came to her as a messenger asking assistance for a sick relative who lived about thirty miles away. She said, "Aunt Mary is very ill and needs you at once. Your father will send you a telegram tomorrow noon and you must go to her."

Mrs. Tuttle evidently accompanied her mother to the home of the sick relative. She saw her aunt lying in bed and observed that it was covered with a quilt having a certain peculiar pattern. She awoke; but had, of course, no means of immediately verifying the dream. About two o'clock on the afternoon of the following day she did receive a telegram from her father conveying the information that her aunt was ill, and requesting her immediate presence. She went, and found her aunt, Mrs. Mary Tinklepaugh, of Sodus, N. Y., very much in need of her assistance, as only a young and inexperienced girl was in charge. Upon entering the sickroom the visitor observed upon the bed a quilt with the pattern she had seen in her dream.

At a much later date Mrs. Tuttle was interested in the project of beautifying the grounds of an estate belonging to a society of which she was a member: Reading in a magazine an announcement that contributions to a tree-planting fund would be received she wrote a letter, enclosing a donation and addressed it to Mrs. R., an officer of the society, but did not get the letter in the mail that evening. That night she dreamed that she visited the estate, over two thousand miles distant, and saw and conversed with several people there. One of them called her attention to the fact that she had addressed the letter to the wrong person, and that if it went to Mrs. R. the money would go into a fund to be used for a totally different purpose. It should, her informant said, be addressed to Mr. W. But the dreamer was not convinced and argued the point. The conversation closed with this advice: "Look again in the magazine and you will see your mistake." In the morning Mrs. Tuttle related her dream to her daughters, and the magazine was looked up. Examination showed that she had been in error in addressing the donation to Mrs. R. and that the dream information was correct.

The letter was re-written and properly addressed. The dream terror of murderers is well known. If our hypothesis is sound the reason is simple, for sleep would again bring the murderer face to face with his victim for the time being. If the murderer be one sensitive enough for the impression to register in the physical brain the experience would be remembered on awakening. If he be less sensitive he might only have a vague sensation of terror instead of the vivid memory of details, as Macbeth apparently did when he referred to "these terrible dreams that shake us nightly." If the murderer be of a very unimpressionable type he would probably be quite undisturbed by anything except physical plane affairs and the fear of legal consequences.

From Providence, R. I., a case is reported in which the dream agony of a murderer led to his arrest. Henry Kelly, seventy years old, was found murdered. The police searched systematically for the perpetrator of the crime but, being unable to find a single clue to the mystery, the case was finally abandoned. Meantime the murderer's remembered astral experiences were so completely destroying his peace of mind that confession was inevitable. One day Frank T. Lyons, twenty-two years old, walked into the police headquarters and surrendered to the authorities. A Providence reporter quotes the self-accused murderer as follows:

"I was haunted by his ghost, and I had to confess. I killed him, though I didn't mean to. Then I went to my room, but I couldn't sleep. I had strange dreams, and in them I saw the old man coming toward me. He seemed to be lame, and to be coming toward me all the time, as if he wanted to say something to me. I couldn't stand it any longer. I fully understand the meaning of this to me. I suppose that it means I will be electrocuted or hanged, but I can't help it. I simply had to tell."

Just how great was the horror created by the "strange dreams" only those who have been able to bring into the waking consciousness astral impressions of the undesirable sort will be able to comprehend. They must, indeed, have been terrible to lead to a confession that might forfeit life, and the sentence; "I couldn't stand it any longer" indicates that the limit of human endurance had been reached. The vivid reality of an astral experience at the moment it comes through into the waking consciousness is such that the just-awakened dreamer sometimes has difficulty, for a moment, in believing that he has not seen the event with the physical eyes. An interesting example of this is reported from Stockholm. It would be well worth while to have the sequel to the story, but it was not possible to follow it up for further details. A press dispatch sent out from Stockholm under date of September 29, 1915, tells the story:

"The identification of a murderer by a man who never saw the prisoner, but who claims to have seen the murder committed in a dream, will be attempted by the local police department just as soon as General Bjorn, who is now critically ill in the west of Sweden, is strong enough to look at the photographs of the anarchist who assassinated his friend General Beckman, on the night of June 26. At the very hour that the crime was committed, but many miles from the scene of it, General Bjorn, raving in delirium, saw in a fever-inspired vision his old friend shot down in a street in Stockholm. Suddenly he shouted: 'Drop that, you scoundrel!' Then: 'The shots are exploding!' When the nurse sought to calm him he became angry and tried to spring out of bed. 'Can't you hear?' he cried. 'Can't you see the smoke? They have murdered General Beckman. Don't you see the blood on the street?' He raved all night, but at daybreak grew calmer and slept an hour. When he woke he said: 'You will find that General Beckman has been murdered. I am sure of it.' He even described the crime in detail. At 9 o'clock the papers arrived telling of the assassination of General Beckman."

Another case in which the details of what is occurring elsewhere are vividly remembered is reported in the Daily Telegram, of Portland, Oregon, of July 2, 1916:

"As he lay dreaming that his brother was dying and that he was vainly trying to restore him, M. E. Lillis, member of the Portland Police Bureau, was awakened by the persistent ringing of the telephone in his home, 565 Hoyt street, this morning. When he awoke and answered, the word came over the wire that his brother, William P. Lillis, special agent of the Portland Railway, Light and Power Company, had died unexpectedly at Seaside at an early hour. When Lillis left for his vacation at

Seaside about a week ago, he was in excellent health, although his constitution had been somewhat weakened by a severe attack of la grippe. It is believed that heart trouble due to the grippe was the cause of death. The body will be shipped to Portland today and funeral arrangements will be made this afternoon."

Three dreams by three people on the same night, and presenting the same details in practically the same language, led to the famous Sutton investigation case at Annapolis. The first chapter of the story is told in a press dispatch from Portland, Oregon, the home of the ill-fated lieutenant's parents, under date of August 11, 1909. It reads:

"Two nights after the tragic death at Annapolis of Lieutenant James M. Sutton, of the United States Marine Corps, each of three women had a dream in which the young man appeared before them and informed them that he had been murdered. 'The son of a gun sneaked up behind me and struck me on the back of the head. The first I knew that I had been shot was when I woke up in eternity.' That is the exact language used by the boy in the dream as he stood before each woman. The persons to whom the young man appeared in dream form are Mrs. J. N. Sutton, his mother, at the family residence in Portland; Mrs. Margaret S. Ainsworth, his aunt, on her farm in Wasco Co., Oregon, and Miss Rose Sutton, his sister, who was then on an Oregon Short Line train speeding to Annapolis. Each woman had the dream Tuesday night, October 15, 1907. Young Sutton died about one o'clock Sunday morning, October 13, 1907."

With this triple corroboration the mother of the dead lieutenant determined to clear her son's name of the suicide charge. Nearly two years passed before she finally had the satisfaction of appearing before the court of inquiry and hearing Dr. Edward M. Shaffer, formerly coroner in the city of Washington, testify that in his opinion as an expert it was quite impossible that Lieutenant Sutton could have fired into his own head the bullet that killed him. After the first dream, and before the official inquiry was held, the mother had other dreams. To a reporter for the San Francisco Examiner, on the eve of the opening of the inquiry August 9, 1909, she said that her dead son had said to her:

"'Mother, dear, don't you believe it. I never killed myself. They beat me to death and then shot me to hide the crime.' He told me how they laid the trap for him, how he walked into it, how one of them grabbed him to pull him out of the automobile, how they held him and beat him; about his forehead being broken; his teeth knocked out, and the lump under his jaw, and how when he was lying on the ground someone kicked him in the side and smashed, his watch. He begged me to live to clear his name. Well, after three weeks I proved some things he told me were true, and after repeatedly demanding the evidence, I got it and within the last month I have proved everything he told me."

An instance in which medical aid was given on account of a dream was told me by Dr. J. S. Devries, now residing at Fremont, Nebraska. In the year of 1898 he was practicing his profession in Fontenelle, Nebraska, and had among his patients the little daughter of Henry Hue, a farmer residing several miles from the town. The doctor, hard driven by a large practice, came home one evening, and retired much exhausted. He had seen his little patient at noon the previous day, and was intending to call again at the same hour on the following day. After sleeping a short time he awoke with an uncertain memory of imminent danger to the little girl, who was afflicted with scarlet fever. While the details were not clear, his apprehension was great, and he felt an irresistible impulse to go to her immediately. Notwithstanding his physical exhaustion, and the complete absence of any tangible evidence that he was needed, he nevertheless ordered his carriage out and drove rapidly to the farmer's home. He arrived at midnight and found the household in commotion, the child exhibiting alarming symptoms, and a messenger just ready to leave to summon him.

Attention has already been called to the fact that one whose physical body is asleep may, in his astral body, visit places at a distance. If his friends are asleep at the same time he may be with them astrally although their sleeping physical bodies may be hundreds of miles apart. If he is asleep, and they are awake he may visit them but could not communicate with them unless they were clairaudient or unless there, were some other method for the interchange of intelligence, such as the planchette, and the waking friend or friends were sufficiently responsive to operate it. A case that illustrates the principles here involved came to my attention soon after its occurrence. A party of six persons, live of whom were my personal friends, were chatting together at the Ansonia Hotel, New York, one evening in June, 1914. The conversation turned to the subject of getting communications from the living by automatic writing. One of the party had had some success in that line, and pencil and paper were procured. Mr. S. thought of Mrs. T., who had sailed for England three days previously, and would therefore be somewhere in mid-ocean. It was then about 10:30 p. m. in New York, and would be well into the night in Mrs. T.'s longitude, and she would presumably be asleep. The group of experimenters got a message about the voyage, and then Mrs. B said to the invisible visitor: "Will you try to remember this experience and put it in a letter to Mr. S. in the morning?" The response, slowly spelled out, was, "I will. Sorry, I have to leave you." About twelve days later Mr. S. received a letter from Mrs. T. which had been written at sea, and was dated on the morning following the experiment. Mrs. T. wrote; "I had a queer experience last night. I suddenly awoke about 2 a. m. The door of my cabin had blown open and was banging. I remembered distinctly of being with you in a circle of people:"

Evidently Mrs. T. could not recall the details of her astral visit. She had no memory of her promise to write a letter about it, but she did remember being with Mr. S. in a circle of people, and this was so unexpected and perplexing that she called it "a queer experience," and felt impelled to write about it. Mr. S. adds that a careful calculation of the variation in time indicates that the hour mentioned by Mrs. T. corresponded with the meeting in New York.

An interesting case of bringing very clearly into the waking consciousness what is transpiring at a distance is a dream of Dr. L. H. Henley, chief surgeon of the Texas and Pacific Railway hospital at Marshall, Texas, who sends me an affidavit with the following story:

"On the morning of January 8, 1910, I awoke about 3 o'clock from a dream about my sister, Mrs. Henry W. Parker, who was living in Randolph Co., N. C. I had not heard from her for some time. I said to my wife, 'Sister Lou is dying- literally choking to death.' Mrs. Henley spoke lightly and reassuringly of the matter. I wrote at once to my sister, inquiring about her health. The following day I received a letter from her that had been written January 7, only a day before my dream occurred, saying that all were well except for severe colds. I showed this letter to my wife, who warned me about being too hasty in telling my dreams! Again at about 3 a. m., January 10, I awakened, and told Mrs. Henley that my sister was dying, sitting in a willow rocking chair, and that her husband, Henry W. Parker, was near death in the adjoining room. This announcement after the very recent letter asserting that the family was well, with the exception of bad colds, led my wife to make some facetious remarks about my sanity.

"No reply ever came to my letter of inquiry, but at 10 a. m., January 16, I received the following telegram:

'Asheboro, N. C, January 15. Dr. L. H. Henley, Marshall,

DREAMS AND PREMONITIONS

Texas. Your sister Lou died Friday and was buried. Henry Parker, her husband, died today. Three children sick and cannot recover. Pneumonia. Come.- Levi V. Lowe.'

"Mr. H. E. Lewis, money order clerk in the post office, Mr. H. E. Behymer and Mrs. Henley were present when the telegram arrived. They had just been joking me about my alarm founded on a dream. I silently handed the telegram about to my friends. I felt quite as certain that the children would not die as I had felt the sad truth about their parents. Later the dream details about my sister's death were verified. The children recovered, and are now living at Edora, Kansas, the two elder ones being Mr. Lindley Parker and Miss Mary Parker."

These dreams have the element of prevision. One of the dreams occurred five days and the other three days before the death of Mrs. Parker, and each of them gave some of the details of her death, as well as the fact that Mr. Parker was near death.

The Messina earthquake, like all great disasters, furnished a number of interesting cases, and one of the best attested was that of the young sailor whose dream revealed to him the spot where his fiance was imprisoned in the ruins, although the most diligent search in his waking consciousness had been unavailing. A press dispatch told the story thus:

"A curious case of rescue was that in which a sailor on board the Italian battleship Regina Elana found his sweetheart. He was granted leave to search for the girl in Messina, with whom he was engaged to be married. After having sought for her in vain for four days in the ruins he returned to the ship exhausted and fell asleep. He dreamed that his fiance said to him, 'I am alive. Come, save me.' On awakening he obtained fresh leave from the commander of the ship, gathered together several friends, and went to the spot of which he had dreamed. The party pried apart the ruins of a house and found the girl uninjured."

If he searched four days in vain he could not have had any particular place in mind where he expected to find her. Yet when he succeeded in bringing the memory of the sleeping hours through into waking consciousness he went immediately to the place where she was imprisoned by the ruins. He not only remembered conversing with the girl, but he evidently had a clear memory of the locality, which enabled him to go to it. The telepathic theorists will hardly venture to argue that he got in telepathic touch with the landscape! Only the hypothesis that the consciousness is functioning in the astral vehicle while the physical body is asleep seems to furnish a satisfactory explanation.

Another case which was widely published also tells the story of a life-saving mission, but under very different circumstances. It occurred in April, 1912, and is given as follows in the press dispatches from Atlanta, Georgia:

"Awakened from a sleep in which he had dreamed that a nearby railway trestle on the Southern Railroad had been washed away, O. T. Kitchens, a section foreman, although suffering from illness, arose from his bed and went to South River, six miles from here, before dawn yesterday, and found that his dream was a reality. The stream, swollen by heavy rains, had carried away a trestle spanning a sixty-five foot chasm. He knew that a passenger train was soon due to arrive at the opposite side of the river, but had no means of reaching that point to warn the engine driver of the danger, and the river is three-quarters of a mile wide. Standing on the bank Kitchens put his hands to his lips and repeatedly shouted for half an hour. Finally he heard an answering shout, and he called out a warning to J. E, Daniel. Daniel flagged the train as it neared the brink of the stream."

How can the advocates of the materialistic hypothesis

possibly explain this? In the Messina case there was the possibility of explaining a part of what occurred by telepathic communication, but in the Kitchens' dream there is no chance whatever of lugging in telepathy. In the other case somebody knew of at least a part of the facts necessary for the rescue.

But here we have a case of a bridge suddenly giving way and imperiling the lives of a trainload of people who knew nothing of the danger that confronted them. Not a human being knew of the collapse of the bridge, not even Daniels, who lived nearby. It was late in the night, towards dawn, and the inhabitants of the countryside were sleeping. Telepathy is absolutely out of the case. There was nobody whose mind contained the information. Kitchens' dream must have been an impelling one. He was ill, and the night was stormy, but in spite of the difficulties in the way his dream resulted in stopping the train, and very probably in saving many lives.

CHAPTER VII

How to Remember Dreams

For the same reason that it is possible to evolve into higher development any faculty or quality which we possess it is also possible to cultivate the art of bringing the memory of our experiences during sleep through into the waking consciousness. But it is of little use for one to attempt it unless one is willing to devote considerable time and thought to it. There is no mystic process by which it can be instantaneously accomplished. We are all familiar with the fact that muscular strength can be developed by almost everybody. But it requires time and attention. A little effort will result in a little muscular gain. But if a man has the ambition to become an athlete he should be willing to put forth patient and long continued exertion in developing physical strength. And just so it is in the matter of evolving the control of the mechanism of consciousness. A little attention to it will be of some value, but one who would fully succeed must resolve in advance to work faithfully at the task.

It seems to be the order of nature that, at the level of evolution represented by the average human being, the activities of consciousness in the waking state, and those of the wider consciousness of the astral realm, shall be separate existences. But as evolution proceeds, and the lessons which can best be learned in the limited physical consciousness are largely acquired, the separating walls slowly dissolve, and ultimately the two states of consciousness are merged in one. When a person has evolved far enough for that happy consummation he no longer "sleeps" in the ordinary meaning of the word. His physical body sleeps, but to his consciousness there is no period of apparent oblivion. He is conscious of lying down to sleep, conscious of his physical body lying on the bed as he moves away from it in his astral body, conscious of all that he sees and

78

hears and does in the ethereal regions during the night, and conscious of his return to his physical body when, in the morning, he takes it up for the activities of the material world once more. His advance in evolution has united the separated fragments that he has called days into a continuous whole, and night has ceased to exist for him, just as it would for one if one could travel rapidly enough to keep always in sight of the sun.

But that marks a fairly high stage in human evolution, and those who have reached it have evolved very desirable mental and moral qualities. The rest of us can at least approximate it, with the requisite effort, and can acquire a sufficient degree of control of the mind and the emotions to bring much more of the astral experiences into the daily life. Those who are willing to take the trouble, and who will be patient and persevering, can have personal proof of the truth of this.

The first step is to control the process of thinking during the waking hours. Most people let the mind wander idly from one thing to another. The current of their thought is directed almost wholly by external things. When the mind is not thus stimulated to action it is likely to get its initiative, quite unconsciously of course, from the mental activity of others in their vicinity- the vagrant thoughts which drift through the brain. Such passive indifference to mental control is fatal to the extension of consciousness. One must learn to think about what one is thinking, and acquire the habit of controlling one's thoughts.

When one begins thus to turn the consciousness back upon itself there comes the opportunity for the ego to make its influence felt in the lower mind. Gradually the mind can thus be brought under control and the connection between the two states of consciousness be strengthened. The truth in that is obvious. Every thoughtful person knows that much thinking about any subject brings knowledge of that subject. It is undoubtedly the natural order of things that the ego, which is the true self, is constantly endeavoring to impress the brain consciousness, is exerting a steady evolutionary pressure, and the degree of success must necessarily be dependent upon the stability of the lower mind.

There are two ways in which the mind receives impressions during sleep- from within and from without. The former are from the ego, and the latter are the vibrations set up by contact with others' vagrant thoughts, or are the automatic action of the brain reproducing its own thought images of the day. If the mind is thus occupied there is little probability that it will be susceptible to the unaccustomed vibrations from the ego. Only when, through thought control during the waking hours, the mind has become responsive to the higher influences, will there be anything from the sleeping state worth remembering.

It then becomes possible for it to register the higher vibrations instead of initiating the lower ones. But mind control alone is not enough. There must also be control of the emotions. The waking thoughts and emotions have a powerful and determining influence upon the activities of the consciousness during the hours when the physical body is asleep. The trivial in thought and the gross in emotion are foreign to the ego and widen the gulf that separates the lower mind from it. The work in hand is to establish the closest possible connection between the two, and success will depend largely upon the extent to which the daily life can be brought into harmony with the life of the ego. Therefore serenity of mind and purity of emotions must be cultivated. While it is important to have this desirable state of mind maintained throughout the waking hours, there is perhaps no other moment of them all that is so essential to success as the instant of falling asleep at night. It seems that the last thought, as one sinks into slumber, has an influence out of all proportion to the time it occupies the mind. By it the trend appears to be given to the mental and emotional activities of the night. If the thought is a sensuous one it seems to attract its gross affinities from its environment, and the mind becomes impervious to higher things. But if the mind is deliberately set upon a pure and lofty theme, as one falls asleep, the channel is open for impressions from the ego which may be recalled upon awakening.

If we reflect a moment upon the fact that there can be no memory of an astral experience unless the delicate vibrations of astral matter have made their impress upon the physical brain, we shall see at once the necessity for the most tranquil and favorable conditions in the lower mind. Worry, and all other forms of mental and emotional disturbance, should be absent. As the instant of sinking into slumber is important so, too, that of awakening is another golden moment to be improved. We are then nearest to the conscious activities of the night, and it is the most propitious time for recalling them. The delicate traces of the astral vibrations are then at their best, but when the physical plane vibrations begin to sweep through the brain the astral impressions may soon be obliterated.

One may write on the smooth sand at the seashore, and it is perfectly legible at the time; but when the tide comes in the boisterous waves erase it and not a trace remains. And so it is with the astral record on the physical brain. The vibrations of the workaday world ordinarily erase them unless they are the record of something that has deeply moved us. Hence the necessity of a little quiet retrospection at the moment of awakening, before the mind has been turned to the business of the waking hours. But while what we can thus recall will help to hold the memory of our astral activities, it is not usually sufficient to anchor it securely in the waking consciousness and, though we may have a vivid recollection when we first awaken, it is extremely likely gradually to fade out until, instead of being able to remember the event, we can only remember that there was something we wished to remember, while every detail of it has vanished in oblivion! Let the reader try the experiment and he will soon discover that the instances in which he can remember throughout the day the dream incidents that were clear in the morning do not constitute the rule, but the exceptions to it.

Now, it is not only the bringing through of the memory into the waking state, but also the retention of the memory that assists one in uniting the two states of consciousness. Means should therefore be employed of anchoring the astral experiences firmly in the mind. This is not so difficult as would at first appear, as the method by which it is accomplished is very simple. It consists merely of writing down the memory upon awakening. If a pad of paper and pencil are left the night before on a stand within easy distance one will soon form the habit of reaching for them with the first gleam of physical consciousness. Indeed, the writing is so frequently begun before the consciousness is in full possession of the physical body that the lines are often difficult to read afterward. But the more immediately it is begun the better. In advance of the experiment it will not seem probable to the beginner that merely having recorded the memory will enable him to retain it if he could not remember it without the memorandum. He will find by experience, however, that with the notes he can readily recall it all, while without them he is quite helpless.

The probability of success in recalling the experiences of the night upon awakening in the morning can be greatly increased by resolving before falling asleep the night before that the moment the waking consciousness returns the memorandum will be made. This pre-resolution may also be used to determine what one shall do during the night in the astral regions. It would appear from careful clairvoyant investigations of the matter, that when a person strongly resolves before going to sleep that he will enter upon a certain course of action he is extremely likely to do so. In this way one may begin to make his nights, as well as his days, useful to others and to himself. He may visit and encourage the ill and the despondent among his living friends and, after sufficient experience, he may have the satisfaction of not only bringing the memory of it through into the waking hours, but also of being able to establish the truth of it by material evidence. One of the simple methods by which this is sometimes done is to write down in the morning a detailed description of some place one has visited often during the sleeping state, but has never seen, or to note the changes that have occurred in some place he has seen- as new buildings erected or trees cut down- and then to verify it all by physically traveling to the place and inspecting it.

If the experimenter is in earnest, and is diligent in his efforts to control h^s mind and emotions, he will in good time achieve at least some degree of success, and that should furnish the motive for farther progress. But he should never fall into the error of believing that because he is beginning to understand the rationale of dreams and is acquiring some accuracy in remembering astral experiences he may therefore safely use his dream consciousness as a guide in physical plane affairs. Of course if there should come to him some warning premonition he will use his common sense in determining what, if anything, he will do. But it would be folly to subordinate the reason to astral impressions and thus set aside sober judgment in deciding upon a course of action. Only when one has succeeded in unifying the physical and astral life to the point where he has no break of consciousness at all when the body sleeps, can he be certain that he may not bring back to the waking state a confused memory. He may, or he may not, correctly translate the astral experiences in the physical brain. He may study the phenomena and he may steadily extend the horizon of his consciousness; but since he cannot positively know whether his memory of a premonition is accurate until the event has occurred, it is obvious that he can only use it for what it may be worth as a suggestion.

An extended discussion of the details of the dream state is beyond the limits of this little volume but there is one characteristic error of translation that deserves attention. The dreamer, by sympathetic association, often merges his consciousness with that of another whom he is observing. Let us say that while in the dream state he sees an accident. A switchman is run down by a locomotive and an arm is cut off. The dreamer upon awakening recalls the scene with himself as chief actor in the accident and, as he remembers it, his own arm was severed. This sympathetic substitution is one of the well established points in dream translation and the student of the subject often finds corroboration of the fact in the public prints.

A case in point is the dream of Mrs. Anderson mentioned in Chapter III. Only brief reference is there made to it but the press reports at the time quoted Mrs. Anderson as saying, "On Thursday morning I had that awful dream. I dreamed we were arguing over papers and I thought I was his wife and would not sign. Then he grabbed me, raised his hand and struck me with a knife." Such substitution seems to be common with untrained observers. One may possibly dream of seeing himself in his own coffin, only because he has in reality seen the funeral of another. Only when he becomes skillful in bringing the memory of his astral experiences through into the waking state can he be certain that no errors are involved.

The element of time is also a cause of confusion. When one has a premonition there is often not the slightest clue to indicate exactly when the event may be expected to occur. This may very possibly be because only fragments of the vision have been brought through into the brain memory. But whatever the cause the fact remains that the event foreseen may occur the next day or may perhaps be far in the future. It is therefore often impossible to base any action upon the information. Such fragmentary and indefinite information is in the same class with the forecast of the future so commonly furnished by the untrained clairvoyant or psychic. It may contain some truth and yet be absolutely inadequate as a basis of action. The point may be illustrated by the experience of one of my friends. He was told that there was a very desirable position for him at the state capitol which he was to fill. This information came to him at a time when his fortunes were at low tide and he was much in need, not so much of "a very desirable position," as of any employment at all that might be secured. Filled with new hope he borrowed a sufficient sum of money for the long journey, went to the capitol building and exhausted every possibility that would lead to the fulfillment of the prophecy. The result was failure and bitter disappointment.

Several years later he was caught up in a popular political movement and was elected lieutenant-governor of the state. He then went to the capitol building for a term of office and the vision of the clairvoyant was justified by the fact.

Among the similar cases that have come under my observation is that of a mining prospector and his partner who were told that great wealth was ahead of them and they went rejoicing to their work. Years of the most commonplace experience followed in which, like thousands of other gold seekers, they managed barely to exist. Finally one of them became discouraged and disgusted and abandoned the enterprise. The other man leased and worked small claims for several more years when, quite unexpectedly, a "pocket" was uncovered and he retired with considerable wealth. Whether or not the clairvoyant really foresaw this denouement the information, as in the instance above given, was misleading and worthless. Thousands of people are continually following the advise of pseudo-psychics to their sorrow, quite overlooking the fact that, although the predictions may often contain some truth, physical affairs cannot usually be directed by them. And precisely so it is with dreams. Their utility lies chiefly in the fact that they disclose to us the real nature of human consciousness. They sometimes give a useful warning, and often furnish much consolation, but, because it is usually impossible for the average person to bring them through into the waking consciousness with accuracy, they can be profitably acted upon only when due allowance has been made for their limitations.

CHAPTER VIII

Dreams of the Dead

Perhaps there is no direction in which the correct understanding of dreams can prove so useful as in relation to our departed friends. Anything that can in some degree lessen the sorrow caused by their absence is certainly worthy of careful study. As a matter of fact the so-called dead are not dead at all, but they are none the less separated from the living or, to put it more accurately, the living are separated from their departed friends; but only because, during the waking hours the consciousness is confined to the physical brain, which is both its instrument and its limitation. During the waking hours the human being is functioning through his astral body plus his physical body, the latter being surrounded and interpenetrated by the matter of the former. When he falls asleep the dense body is left behind. He is then functioning through his astral body, which is what the miscalled dead are also doing. The living and the "dead" are, therefore, again together. If, fortunately, the bereaved person remembers it in the morning, he thinks he has had a dream.

Now, since dreams are of two kinds- memories of astral experiences and memories of impressions caused by the automatic activity of the physical brain and its etheric counterpart- this memory of the departed may be either the one or the other. If the cause of the dream is the brain pictures, they are likely to be related to scenes through which the dreamer has recently passed, possibly the events of the last days of the departed. If the dream is the memory of an astral experience, a visit to the departed- it is likely to be more vivid and realistic. In such a case the experience is life-like, the time passes joyously and the dreamer often awakens with a feeling of blissful exaltation, for he has really been with the loved one and the joy he has felt is reflected in the waking consciousness.

Unfortunately, with the person, who does not understand the facts as they are, this uplifting emotion is immediately quenched by the gloomy belief that it is all a fantasy of the brain. This belief is unfortunate for more than one reason. It prevents the dreamer cultivating the art of bringing the memory of such association more fully into the waking state, while the depression of the bereaved person acts disastrously upon the one who is mourned as dead and lost. It is, of course, natural that the belief that one is separated from those he loves for the remainder of this life should cause great sorrow. If the fact were known that the separation is only on the part of the one who remains behind, and that that is confined to the hours of waking consciousness, the grief would be greatly modified. To know that whether we remember it or not, whether we dream or do not dream, we are always with the departed during the hours of sleep, if there is an attracting tie of love between us, would soon bring permanent serenity instead of the hopeless despair that is so common and so unfortunate for everybody concerned. Depressing emotions are bad enough for the living but very much worse for those for whom they mourn. As the physical body is the instrument of action, the astral body is the vehicle of emotion. In the waking state an emotion arises in the astral body and passes outward into the physical mechanism, a large percentage of its energy being exhausted in setting the physical particles in motion.

Consequently emotions are very much keener in the astral life than in the physical. It is no exaggeration to say that a given cause will produce a very great deal more of either joy or sorrow in the astral life than in the physical. Therefore when bereaved people give way to unrestrained sorrow and despair they are doing the worst thing possible for their departed friends. We have only to reflect upon the fact that we are all more or less affected by the elation and the depression of people about us to understand that emotions are contagious. Persons who habitually indulge that form of depression commonly known as "the blues" are injuriously affecting all who come near them in proportion to the sensitiveness of their victims. Life may thus be made quite miserable for those who are extremely sensitive. Multiply that effect many times and it will give some idea of the disastrous results to their "dead" friends of the grief and despair of which they are the helpless cause.

Such mourning, in the last analysis, is not on account of any fate that awaits them but is caused by our sense of personal loss; and when we reflect upon the fact that such grief on our part brings still greater sorrow to them the value of a knowledge of the facts becomes apparent. There is but one sensible attitude to assume toward those who have passed on. We should think of them as cheerfully as possible and never with longing regret and the desire that they should be with us again. They are with us every night that we sleep and a little patient consideration of that fact will be likely to bring to most people an increasing serenity and joy.

If people were better able to bring accurate memories of astral experiences into the waking life it would no doubt often be of the greatest satisfaction to those who have passed over to the other life as well as to the dreamer. There are a number of cases on record in which those who have passed on suddenly, without leaving full information about their affairs behind them, have endeavored for a long time to pass such knowledge back before they succeeded. Who shall say how many never succeed at all? The Reeves Snyder case and the Moore case, in Chapter III, are examples of the recovery of valuables which, especially in the Moore case, would probably have been forever lost to the surviving relatives but for the fortunate dream. It was more than two years after the death of Mr. Moore that the buried coin was recovered. Who can guess how long he had been endeavoring to reveal the hiding place of the little fortune to his wife and what he suffered by the long delay, and the fear that his failure to impart the information at the time the money was secreted might be the cause of continued poverty?

Very much of the heartache caused by death would disappear if the truth about the "dead" were known and the facts about sleep and dreams were understood. The least that we can do for our part is to recognize the relationship that exists in consciousness between our departed friends and ourselves and, by study of the facts and by serious efforts at the control of the mind and the emotions, bring about the conditions that will enable us to get much consolation from the truth instead of remaining ignorant of it.

THE END

Made in the USA
Middletown, DE
29 January 2023

23466391R00056